ENJOYING THE PRESENCE OF GOD

DISCOVERING INTIMACY WITH GOD IN THE DAILY RHYTHMS OF LIFE

JAN JOHNSON

NAVPRESS

BRINGING TRUTH TO LIFE

NavPress Publishing Group

P.O. Box 35001, Colorado Springs, Colorado 80935

OUR GUARANTEE TO YOU

We believe so strongly in the message of our books that we are making this quality guarantee to you. If for any reason you are disappointed with the content of this book, return the title page to us with your name and address and we will refund to you the list price of the book. To help us serve you better, please briefly describe why you were disappointed. Mail your refund request to: NavPress, P.O. Box 35002, Colorado Springs, CO 80935.

The Navigators is an international Christian organization. Our mission is to reach, disciple, and equip people to know Christ and to make Him known through successive generations. We envision multitudes of diverse people in the United States and every other nation who have a passionate love for Christ, live a lifestyle of sharing Christ's love, and multiply spiritual laborers among those without Christ.

NavPress is the publishing ministry of The Navigators. NavPress publications help believers learn biblical truth and apply what they learn to their lives and ministries. Our mission is to stimulate spiritual formation among our readers.

© 1996 by Jan Johnson
All rights reserved. No part of this publication may be reproduced in any form without written permission from NavPress, P.O. Box 35001, Colorado Springs, CO 80935.
    www.navpress.com
Library of Congress Catalog Card Number: 96-7022
ISBN 08910-99263

Inset photograph: PhotoDisk

Cover photograph: Russell Kord/H. Armstrong Roberts, Inc.

Some of the anecdotal illustrations in this book are true to life and are included with the permission of the persons involved. All other illustrations are composites of real situations, and any resemblance to people living or dead is coincidental.

Unless otherwise identified, all Scripture quotations in this publication are taken from the *HOLY BIBLE: NEW INTERNATIONAL VERSION* ® (NIV®). Copyright © 1973, 1978, 1984 by International Bible Society. Used by permission of Zondervan Publishing House. All rights reserved. Other versions used include: the *Revised Standard Version Bible* (RSV), copyright 1946, 1952, 1971, by the Division of Christian Education of the National Council of the Churches of Christ in the USA, used by permission, all rights reserved; *The Living Bible* (TLB), © 1971 owned by assignment by the Illinois Regional Bank N.A. (as trustee), used by permission of Tyndale House Publishers, Inc., Wheaton, IL 60189; *The Jerusalem Bible*, © 1966 by Darton, Longman & Todd, Ltd., and Doubleday & Company, Inc. All rights reserved; *The Message* (MSG), Copyright 1993, 1994, 1995, 1996 by Eugene Peterson, used by permission of NavPress Publishing Group; and the *King James Version* (KJV).

Johnson, Jan, 1947-
    Enjoying the presence of God : discovering intimacy with God in the daily rhythms of life / Jan Johnson.
      p.   cm.
    ISBN 0-89109-926-3
    1. Christian life. 2. God—Worship and love. I. Title.
BV4501.J565 1996
248.4—dc20   96-7022
                                                  CIP

Printed in the United States of America

4 5 6 7 8 9 10 11 12 13 14 15 / 05 04 03 02

FOR A FREE CATALOG OF
NAVPRESS BOOKS & BIBLE STUDIES,
CALL 1-800-366-7788 (USA)
or 1-416-499-4615 (CANADA)

Contents

Words of praise for *Enjoying the Presence of God*:

"For many of us, experiencing God's presence is hard work. This book shows us how to relax and enjoy God in the everyday activities of life."
—Dr. Christine Aroney-Sine, medical consultant in international health and author of *Tales of a Seasick Doctor*

"What we need are simple, practical, clear suggestions on how to practice God's presence. Enjoying the Presence of God *shows us many possible paths to explore as we look to our Shepherd and walk with Him."*
—Pamela Reeve, professor and advisor of Women's Ministries, Multnomah Bible College & Biblical Seminary; conference speaker; and author of *Faith Is . . .*

"Are you weary of performance-oriented and shame-based approaches to Christian spirituality? Enjoying the Presence of God *is a refreshing alternative. It is full of encouragement and practical wisdom. I highly recommend it."*
—Dale Ryan, CEO, Christian Recovery International

Dedicated to the careful, rarely named journalist,
Abbé Joseph de Beaufort,
who interviewed Brother Lawrence,
recorded their conversations,
gathered his letters, and turned the material into the book,
The Practice of the Presence of God

1

Trying Too Hard

I used to have dazzling quiet times. I sat on my bed, holding my four-part prayer notebook as if it were a cherished artifact. Pulling back the tab marked "adoration," I peered at a list of forty words that described God and picked three to praise God for. Moving on to the tab marked "confession," I mulled over another forty-word list of faults, especially those I'd underlined in red: laziness and grouchiness. Racing on to "thanksgiving," I skimmed a list of twenty items I felt thankful for, including friends, relatives, books, and—to be especially spiritual—God Himself.

At the bottom of the page, a stretching zinger challenged me: Thank God for one thing you've never thanked Him for before.

Finally, I had enough momentum to slide into home plate—a list of requests I had kept for ten years: former students, weight control, missionary friends. It took quite a while to do this portion of the notebook, but when I finished, I felt as if I'd covered the map with God.

My quiet time in those days was crisp and thorough, tight

and structured. You would have expected this from me—a Bible study leader, a throaty alto in the church choir, an armchair counselor to those who felt at odds with life. I was a doer in life—even in my relationship with God.

In spite of my spiritual whiz-kid persona, I was crumbling and raging inside. I felt suffocated by the routine life of a stay-at-home mom, the impossibility of church work, and the dry ache of a vanishing marriage. I remember the day my quiet time died. After gathering all my devotional props, I settled into a terrible emptiness. I needed God as I had never needed Him before, but my regimented prayers were puny containers for my anguish. Hurling my prayer notebook across the room, I asked myself, *How would I survive life without someone to love me? How could I connect with God so that no matter what happened to me, I would believe that God still loved me and valued me? What would replace these sterile lists so I could sink my teeth into a God who would satisfy my neediness?*

> *I remember the day my quiet time died. After gathering all my devotional props, I settled into a terrible emptiness. I needed God as I had never needed Him before, but my regimented prayers were puny containers for my anguish.*

As my ego props fell away—ministry positions, marriage security—I replaced my sterling quiet time with reading *Glamour* magazine. I found refuge in food and snacked all day. Appalled that my secret food compulsion was taking over, I slithered into a room with other "losers" like me—a support group for compulsive eaters. When I said I was "fine," they laughed and said, "Right! So how are you really doing?" My Christian facade, which I didn't know I had, cracked.

Over several years, these meetings schooled me in admitting the truth—that I demanded perfection from myself and everyone around me. I saw that I had behaved as a Pharisee, "the one who wants to get the right formula and do it right and fix everything and feel very wonderful."[1]

But I found it difficult to forget about dazzling God and

show Him my real self. Finally, as I meandered through the Psalms, I found comfort in their honest and gritty texture:

> I sink in the miry depths,
>> where there is no foothold.
> I have come into the deep waters;
>> the floods engulf me.
> I am worn out calling for help;
>> my throat is parched.
> My eyes fail,
>> looking for my God. (Psalm 69:2-3)

Were I as honest as the psalmist, I'd have to admit that I had been mad at God—why hadn't He fixed everything and put my life in order as I'd wanted it? Could I admit to God that I felt I was a disappointment to Him, and He was a disappointment to me? In a moment of terror I did, and the sky didn't fall.

I still felt broken, but somehow hopeful. It seemed as if God were wringing all that self-sufficiency out of me and asking me to seek Him in whatever way He led me. He wasn't going to fix my life quickly, but He was going to mold my character. At the time, I couldn't see it, but God was showing me that He did not want me to be a can-do go-getter but "one who becomes broken bread and poured out wine in the hands of Jesus Christ."[2]

I began a journey that looks as though it will take my entire life: to relish being God's much-loved child instead of trying to be wonderful; to accept my inability to control people and circumstances and surrender them to God. I switched roles: I chose to be the defeated prodigal son who "came to himself" instead of the dutiful older brother looking for rewards. I decided to head home to the Parent who loves me no matter what—even when I fail.

But in this new path of "being" instead of "doing," how was I going to relate to God in a way that wasn't so busy, so ordered, so perfect? Not with my old methods of prayer—I could no longer blitz through the prayer requests in my notebook. Wasn't there a simpler way of praying that wasn't so struc-tured, that allowed me to express the contradictions of the heart? But what? I needed a new approach entirely. I couldn't exchange one brand of performance for another.

I recalled having read a small book that recorded the ideas of Brother Lawrence: *The Practice of the Presence of God*. This sounded fun and interesting compared to my Olympic-style quiet time. It was so low-key I could never spiff it up into some ego-strutting routine.

As I experimented with unpretentious, plain-speaking con-versation with God, the adventure began. God wasn't squinting down at me from His Supreme Court chair waiting to see if I mentioned every name on my request list. He was sitting next to me on the backyard swing, eager to hear me, waiting me out, offering me cues.

At first, I was baffled about what to do. Then I'd remind myself: this isn't a method but a relationship. As I read more of the devotional classics (books written about the devotional life that have stood the test of time), I came to understand that bullying and berating myself with "shoulds" and "oughts" hin-dered my awareness of God rather than helped it. I had to be patient. Desire for God would not flow out of me effortlessly, sincerely, and spontaneously by next Tuesday. Day by day, though, I would develop a "familiar friendship with Jesus,"[3] in which I could trust Him with my secret flaws, deepest fears, and hidden dreams.

This kinder, gentler approach had an ordinariness about it exemplified by Brother Lawrence's non-hero status.[4] This earthy fellow (whose name was Nicholas Herman) was a lay brother with the barefooted Carmelites in Paris in 1666. Lowly and unlearned, he had served as a soldier and household ser-vant. He wasn't a scholar — doctrinal debates bored him. He worked in the monastery and called himself "a servant of the servants of God." An overweight bumbler and "great awkward fellow, who broke everything,"[5] he worshiped more in the kitchen than in the cathedral. He wrote:

10

The time of business does not with me differ from the time of prayer, and in the noise and clatter of my kitchen, while several persons are at the same time calling for different things, I possess God in as great tranquility as if I were upon my knees.[6]

I could imagine the sauce simmering and Brother Lawrence tripping over the monastery cat, yet still enjoying the companionship of God. This was the path to God I longed to travel.

I had complicated the spiritual life with my notebook and checklists and invented my own version of "spiritual correctness." In truth, I needed only one thing—God. I didn't need a great quiet time, I needed a God-centered lifetime. I saw that my responsibility as a Christian was to seek God's company, not to seek spiritual maturity.

> *In truth, I needed only one thing—God. I didn't need a great quiet time, I needed a God-centered lifetime.*

Enjoying God's presence offered a quieter, playful pathway to God, void of my quest for righteousness. I dabbled in authentic prayer, "the place where we can be completely ourselves,"[7] where God welcomes faults, gifts, and laughter. I had spent years trying to be too spiritual, too advanced, too wonderful. I saw in Brother Lawrence that people can follow hard after God in ways that don't appear spiritual at all: "He had often passed his time appointed for prayer in rejecting wandering thoughts and falling back into them"; "he could never regulate his devotion by certain methods as some do."[8]

∞

For several years now, I've stood before God making no promises to achieve, only that I would attempt and enjoy this gentle pattern. I keep asking God this question and making this choice:

Can I bring God back in my mind-flow every few seconds so that God shall always be in my mind as an after image, shall always be one of the elements in every

11

concept and precept? I choose to make the rest of my
life an experiment in answering this question.[9]

This book is a small attempt to record experiments by
Christians who have kept company with God. I invite you to
seek God and enjoy His presence, but I don't want to prescribe
a method. I want to introduce you to so many possibilities for
enjoying God's presence that you will find your own—especially the ways God is already cultivating in your life.

QUESTIONS TO PONDER,
EXPERIMENTS TO CONSIDER

In what ways do you work at your relationship with God? If
"work" doesn't describe your efforts, what word does? Why?

———

How do you feel about having a "quiet time"? How have your
quiet times worked out?

CHAPTER

2

Practicing the Presence of God

Alicia squints as she perches on her stool and peers at the circuit board in front of her. With skilled finesse, she inserts wire no bigger than her breath into holes no one else can see. Sometimes the work at this electronics firm seems boring to her, but sensing God's companionship in the middle of it all makes it more interesting.

In the milliseconds between staring at charts and duplicating their images on the circuit board, Alicia looks over at her sister at the next work station. Her sister is grieving over her relationship with her husband. *Show me if I can help*, Alicia prays. She nods an affirming yes, relieved that she can at least pray for her sister.

As Alicia begins another task, she quizzes God, *What shall we talk about while I work?* Her eyes scan the room until she spots a calendar at someone's work station with these words printed on it, "Pray for the harvest, for the laborers are few." Unsure of exactly which laborers she's praying for, Alicia sits in the mystery of that verse for the rest of the afternoon as she earns an hourly wage that buys gas for the family van and shoes for the children.

The next day when Alicia walks into the bathroom at work, she sees the newest member of the crew walking with a group of women who have made fun of Alicia for her Spanish accent. Alicia feels disappointed that this new woman has fallen into such careless company. Then Alicia sees brochures pass from the woman's hand into the other women's hands. The woman is talking to them about God!

Alicia leans over the bathroom sink and pats her face with water: "So, God," she says, laughing, "I guess this woman is the laborer I've been praying for."

> *An awareness of God can flow through our day the way blood circulates through the body, replenishing it with nutrients and oxygen.*

An awareness of God can flow through our day the way blood circulates through the body, replenishing it with nutrients and oxygen. We pay attention to God, conscious that He may be speaking to us. His presence begins to permeate our lives—through thoughts, feelings, dreams, activities, and in-between moments.

Practicing God's presence moves His companionship beyond church gatherings, before-meal graces, and quiet times to infiltrate the ordinary moments of life. Keeping company with God this way transforms tasks such as building circuit boards into acts of worship because we know at whose feet we sit for the rest of our lives.

REMINDING US WHO WE ARE

From God's perspective, enjoying His presence is perfectly natural—not lofty or difficult. God created us out of love and stamped us with His image. He chose for Himself the role of parent, relishing human companionship as pictured by His walking in the cool of the day with Adam and Eve in a young creation. God delights in us and wants us to connect with who He is:

> "But let him who boasts boast about this:
>   that he *understands and knows me,*

that I am the LORD, who exercises kindness,
   justice and righteousness on earth,
     for in these I *delight,*" declares the LORD.
         (Jeremiah 9:24, emphasis added)

Prayer isn't a performance, but a "climbing up to the heart of God,"[1] as Martin Luther said. Enjoying God's presence places us squarely in God's lap, where He enjoys us:

The LORD your God is with you, . . .
He will take great delight in you,
   he will quiet you with his love,
   he will rejoice over you with singing.
     (Zephaniah 3:17)

This awareness of God's presence is part of how we delight in God, which we are commanded to do: "Delight yourself in the LORD and he will give you the desires of your heart" (Psalm 37:4). Frequently, this verse is hijacked as a formula for getting what we want from God: If you delight in God, God rewards you with your heart's desires. We misunderstand the possibility that delighting in the Lord is the thing that fulfills the desires of the heart. Brother Lawrence put it this way: "Our only business was to love and delight ourselves in God."[2]

This delight moves us toward the eternal goal, according to Revelation, of living eternally in the full presence of God by worshiping Him. In the here-and-now, it speeds us toward the goal of coming to "know Christ and the power of his resurrection" (Philippians 3:10), of coming to "know and rely on the love God has for us" (1 John 4:16). In the flurry of daily events, the back-and-forth pulse of our conversation with God can bring us home to these truths about who we are and what we were created for.

WHY WE HESITATE

Some wonder if it's possible to practice God's presence at all times. It must be possible in some sense, for the apostle Paul urged us to "pray in the Spirit on all occasions with all kinds of prayers and requests" (Ephesians 6:18). In Scripture, the words *always* and *prayer* appear together often:

> Epaphras . . . is *always wrestling in prayer* for you, that you may stand firm in all the will of God, mature and fully assured. (Colossians 4:12, emphasis added)

> We always thank God for all of you, *mentioning you in our prayers.* (1 Thessalonians 1:2, emphasis added)

> Do not be anxious about anything, but *in everything, by prayer and petition,* with thanksgiving, present your requests to God. (Philippians 4:6, emphasis added)

Paul emphasized the continual nature of his prayers by saying that his companions prayed night and day for the Thessalonians (1 Thessalonians 3:10). Prayer became "the main business of their lives."[3]

But isn't this more than we could possibly hope to achieve? "We are not incessantly making vocal prayers, but our heart is always turned toward God, always listening for the voice of God, always ready to do His holy will,"[4] explained eighteenth-century Jesuit priest Jean Nicholas Grou. Quaker author Douglas Steere adds: "When a young man is in love with a girl, he does not think of his beloved every instant if he has important work to do. But his devotion to her permeates all that he does with an overtone, and when a pause comes his mind naturally turns to the loved object."[5]

Besides, this is not something we do, but something God does in us. It isn't a matter of achieving God's presence, but surrendering to God's presence that is already within the Christian. It's more than a habit, it's a fundamental way of living. As a flag or banner waves over a castle continuously, the presence of God hovers around us, sometimes rippling in the wind, other times resting quietly, but always in a place that stands out, that cannot escape the eyes we are training to recognize Him.

Do we have to be a serene, mystical type to try this? No, personality is not a factor. Alicia is a fun-loving mischief-maker, the playful joker among her sisters. Even those who burned out as I did can slip into this practice. Our charred edges motivate us to mutter to God about the people and circumstances we want to control (but can't), and these murmurs are seeds helping us begin to pay attention to a God who is always there. They sprout as we let God's presence satisfy the hunger inside us.

Although personality isn't a factor, character is. It is necessary to set aside the idea that spirituality is something one can achieve. Gifts, goals, and talents as well as flaws, failures, and problems must be surrendered to God, who treasures us with our flaws and works through them. Without this surrendering of life, someone might trade in a works-oriented quiet time for an equally frantic constant conversation with God. Instead, performance is replaced by surrender, and self-consciousness gives way to self-forgetfulness. Enjoying God's presence means we stop trying to prove ourselves to God and decide to love Him and enjoy Him forever.

> *This is not something we do, but something God does in us. It isn't a matter of achieving God's presence, but surrendering to God's presence that is already within the Christian.*

Perhaps you think this sounds so inward, so directed toward me, myself, and I. Oddly enough, a practiced awareness of God's presence doesn't pull people into themselves, it pushes the attention outward. It gives us eyes to see the world differently and to become self-forgetful about our service. We discover that God is most glorified in us when we are most satisfied in Him.[6]

Keeping company with God is so down-to-earth and natural that many people already do this without realizing it. Whose thoughts haven't wandered toward God in deep contemplation in the car? Who hasn't dug into the earth in the garden and felt the joy of being closely connected with God's creation? Much of life already is interaction with God, but we don't know it. We are like Sleeping Beauty—the prince has kissed us, but we don't wake up.

17

Perhaps enjoying God's presence sounds too facile, too uncomplicated to be worth much. This is especially true if you've spent a lot of time trying to impress God with your earnest performance as a Christian. But "[God] is never impressed by earnestness,"[7] wrote Oswald Chambers, and this is evidenced by the way Jesus talked about prayer with child-like simplicity. When the disciples asked Jesus to teach them "to pray"—not "how to pray" (see Luke 11:1)—He modeled prayer instead of giving them elaborate how-to instructions. Our grand experiment begins the same way. Instead of worrying about how to do it right, we plunge in and try.

But we're uneasy. What do we do? What is the agenda? We do as the disciples did—ask Christ to teach us. Peace penetrates the relationship when we are content to waste time with God and rest in His presence. There's no need to impress God with long lists of requests or complicated prayer notebooks. This sort of formula-based spirituality teaches us to follow other people's paths to God, rather than developing our own relationship with Him. Following the current trend in quiet times or devotional reading can cause us to bypass genuine engagement with God. We are better off to accept Jean Nicholas Grou's gentle challenge, "Love God, and you will always be speaking to Him,"[8] and see what happens.

LIMITED VIEWS OF PRACTICING GOD'S PRESENCE

Thinking About God All the Time
Thinking and reasoning play a large part in our spiritual growth, and the Bible emphasizes the importance of having our thoughts renewed (Romans 8:6, 12:2; 1 Corinthians 2:16). It's a mistake, however, to limit enjoying God's presence to mental activity only.

Our rational Western culture has convinced us that spirituality is mostly an intellectual pursuit. God is sometimes compared to a giant computer, and we are supposedly microprocessors of the Great Main Frame. Because many of us work at information-based jobs in which we live in our heads all day—analyzing, sorting, and projecting—we try, without realizing it, to *think* our way into heaven. We constantly search for new facts. Studying about God in periodic classes crowds out the idea of dwelling with God for endless moments.

With this mind-set, enjoying God's presence seems to occur only while engaged in thought at church or Bible studies. It seems unusual, maybe even funny, to consider God's presence in the parts of our lives that are not necessarily intellectual pursuits—dreaming, eating, playing sports. Paying attention to God's presence is wider and deeper than thinking about God all the time. It involves the ordinary activities of our entire being—feeling, sensing, listening, and moving in such a way that watering plants, playing volleyball, and walking on the beach take on a rhythm of prayer.

Feeling Warm Toward God

When we aren't longing for new and improved insights about God, we're eager for warm feelings from God and complain if "magic moments" seldom occur. Enjoying God's presence encompasses feelings, but it's bigger than that. It is living in the reality that "God is closer to us than we are to ourselves."[9]

Some doubt God's constant presence when they don't feel it. The truth is that God is always present because Christ promised to be present with us: "Lo, I am with you alway" (Matthew 28:20, KJV). God is present everywhere at the same time (Psalm 139:2-7). As we learn to pay attention to that presence, we may notice Him more often. It isn't wise, however, to worry about feeling good, because then we're focusing on ourselves again instead of letting go and living in the awareness of God's presence.

Intense feelings do sometimes occur in our conversations with God, but God-man conversations in the Bible were more terrifying than tingling. Moses went through a desperate self-search while standing in front of the burning bush; Jacob's visceral encounter with the Lord—a wrestling match—left him with a limp. God's conversations with people in the Bible had an ordinariness about them. God and Abraham talked about the covenant again and again just as friends often rehash important events over and over.

As we consider enjoying the presence of God, we must avoid the cultural traps of Western Christianity, which is hooked on knowing God through these two avenues only:

- information and facts
- inspiration and feelings

By inviting God to dwell in *every* part of ourselves—will, imagination, intuition, body, and sense of humor—we can enjoy intimacy with Him more easily. The Russian mystic Theophan the Recluse described well the interplay going on inside us and the atmosphere it creates: "To pray is to descend with the mind into the heart, and there to stand before the face of the Lord, ever-present, all-seeing, within you."[10]

EXPERIMENTERS

If you're interested in continuing this adventure, consider yourself an experimenter. As a researcher, you're not out to impress anyone or achieve anything, but to explore what it means to enjoy God's presence. Little has been written about it, so there are no how-to lists or exhaustive guidelines. We *practice* the presence of God—we attempt it, work out the kinks, and then try it some more. Frank Laubach, an early-1900s missionary to the Philippines, experimented with practicing the presence of God and reported this experience:

> I was on a Pennsylvania train praying at the back of a woman's head with a picture of Hoffman's "Boy Christ" in my hand, when she suddenly turned around and said, "What the world needs is more religion."
> "Are you a missionary?" I asked her.
> "No," she said, "my husband is the conductor."
> "You must be a very religious woman," I said.
> "No," she replied, "I am a Methodist, but I don't do much at it."

"Then why," I asked, "did you say the world needs more religion?"

"I don't know," she replied, "but I just felt like talking about it."

Something of this kind is an everyday occurrence with us who pray for everybody we meet. It never happens unless we are praying.[11]

This experiment in keeping constant company with God cannot be rushed because God is doing the work in us and we cannot hurry God. We let go of the desire to perform and ease into this practice, knowing that intimacy is never instant. We are embarking on a lifelong journey of welcoming the invasion of our soul by the Holy Spirit so that moments with God are sprinkled throughout the day like manna in the desert.

QUESTIONS TO PONDER, EXPERIMENTS TO CONSIDER

Consider asking God to show you if there are ways you already practice His presence without realizing it.

———

Think of a place in which you are usually bored, and consider praying for someone or some circumstance nearby. For example, waiting in a doctor's office can prompt us to pray for the doctors and medical personnel or for patients receiving bad news or even for integrity in medical research.

———

Consider for a moment what might have motivated the disciples to ask Jesus to teach them to pray (Luke 11:1). What motivates you?

3

Thinking About You Becomes Praying for You

I hadn't seen Lynne for several months. Five years before, she and her husband had divorced after he revealed that he was gay. His ministry in a large church crumbled and their financial status plunged. "During these five years," she told me, "I've been most angry that he's never given me even ten dollars for our three girls. So this is what I did. I took one of his shirts to a barbecue pit on the beach and set it on fire with a blowtorch. I wanted to celebrate that I had forgiven him just a little bit."

This was forgiveness? I thought.

"I've gotten rid of a little more of the anger," she continued. "I've discovered that forgiveness doesn't happen all at once. Maybe Jesus said to forgive seventy times seven because we'd have to forgive some people every time we think about them. Every time I think of him, I forgive him a little more. I'd finally forgiven him a certain amount—that's why I celebrated."

Lynne's words, "Every time I think of him, I forgive him a little more," forged for me another small path for abiding in God's presence—offering a brief prayer every time I thought of someone. Instead of forming opinions of people—"How disgusting he is!" or "How clever she is!"—I could pray for that person. Perhaps the apostle Paul had a similar practice of praying for people when he thought of them, evidenced by his words, "I thank my God every time I remember you" (Philippians 1:3).

BREATH PRAYERS

Our back-and-forth communication with God might take the time-proven "breath prayer" format, repeating a familiar prayer of nine or ten syllables or less that has great meaning. To those of us who have spent our energies reciting long lists of prayer requests, breath prayers may seem hackneyed and infantile, but they aren't. Breath prayers are so simple that they're revolutionary. In his book *A Testament of Devotion*, Quaker pastor and college professor Thomas Kelly says this about breath prayers: "The processes of inward prayer do not grow more complex,

> *What a relief to grow into a relationship with God where we don't have to go on and on explaining everything. We can rest in the confidence that God already knows and understands.*

but more simple. . . . We begin with simple, whispered words. Formulate them spontaneously, 'Thine only. Thine only.' Or seize upon a fragment of the Psalms: 'so panteth my soul after Thee, O God.' Repeat them inwardly, over and over again."[1]

As the fictional character Mary Lindsay in *The Scent of Water* found her way back to God, she stumbled upon these breath prayers: "Into Thy hands," "Lord, have mercy," and "Thee I adore."[2] The first one, "Into Thy hands," helps us relinquish to God our fear, our anguish, and our desire to control:

- I am afraid of upcoming surgery — Into Thy hands.
- I don't want my church to split — Into Thy hands.
- I want this person to love me, but he doesn't — Into Thy hands.

Yes, it's too simple, but what a relief to grow into a relationship with God where we don't have to go on and on explaining everything. We can rest in the confidence that God already knows and understands.

We need this simplicity in a culture that wows people with words—adorning them with graphics, manipulating and convincing people with words. Breath prayers resemble the unembellished approach Jesus recommended when He spoke of offering a simple yes or no instead of elaborate oaths (Matthew 5:33-37).

Breath prayers are very different from "vain repetitions," which Jesus described as lofty, impressive recitations made for others to notice (Matthew 6:7, KJV). They are quiet groanings of the heart that become more meaningful as we use them. As we turn these prayers over and over, they become woven through these thoughts and may even transform our attitudes.

You probably have breath prayers that you already use, but you don't call them that. Here are some that may spark your thinking.

Turn this person's heart toward You. This breath prayer paraphrases biblical statements about God's power to change motives and attitudes (1 Kings 8:58, Psalm 119:36, Luke 1:17). Whether we're miffed at a government official or crusty old Aunt Franny, this breath prayer keeps us focused on God's will in the person's life. Sometimes I add, *Turn my heart toward this person,* as a prayer to empty myself of my well-researched opinion of his or her behavior. These prayers can wring the self-importance from our attitude and allow God to put within us the most loving attitude we can muster.

Do I need to change? Disturbing people or situations may signal us to look within for character flaws (1 Corinthians 11:28, 2 Corinthians 13:5). Asking if we need to change lets the issue simmer on the back burner until God makes it plain whether we need to change or to turn over the thing that disturbs us.

Teach me through this negative behavior. Rather than dwelling on the inadequacies of people we find offensive, this breath prayer helps us refocus on God's desire to transform us. We ponder, *What does this person's negative example teach me about myself? What warning does his or her behavior present?* Using this breath prayer on a regular basis also rescues us from our self-righteousness—the plague of those who seek God—and calls us back to the reality that we are all flawed learners.

Thank You for this person. People who have contributed to our lives fly across our thoughts many times, and a smile of thanks can be a pleasant breath prayer.

Spontaneous breath prayers often spring from our study of Scripture. For several months, I meditated on Matthew 5:17-48, searching for clues about what it meant to be tender-hearted. That one word, "tenderhearted," became a breath prayer. In this way, breath prayers become valuable tools to help God's Word reverberate within our inner selves.

Don't be afraid of playful breath prayers that some might call inside jokes between God and you. My playful rejoinder to God when He seems to outdo Himself—rescuing a friend from bankruptcy or helping an addict friend go straight—is, "Now I believe!" This grew out of meditating on the passage in which the father of the possessed boy exclaimed, "I do believe; help me overcome my unbelief!" (Mark 9:24). Like that father, I believe, but not enough, and God keeps strengthening my belief. It's fun to tell God when we believe just a little more.

Scripture lends itself especially to what might properly be called a litany rather than a breath prayer. A litany is a longer, memorized prayer that has a chantlike quality to it. On a recent business trip, I scheduled too much in too little time, which was not as conducive to enjoying God's presence as I had become accustomed. To keep all my appointments, my plane had to land on time and I had to rent a car quickly, drive across town in a few minutes, and then drive to another meeting in a few more minutes. I had been nervous about it for days, but when my plane landed I finally began resting in Isaiah 26:3: "Thou wilt keep him in perfect peace, whose mind is stayed on thee: because he trusteth in thee" (KJV). Trying to read the tiny print on the street map, I acknowledged God's presence with this breath prayer: "Thou wilt keep, and keep, and keep."

WHEN WE DON'T KNOW WHAT TO PRAY

As we learn to surrender people to God each time we think of them, certain people confuse or overwhelm us. We're stumped. For example, the first time I tried to pray for a stranger as Frank Laubach prayed for the woman on the train, I couldn't think of anything to pray. The simplest solution is to ask God to show us what to pray. In the meantime, we can borrow phrases from biblical prayers. The following phrases are a start:

- Help this person come to know Christ and the power of His resurrection (Philippians 3:10).
- Help this person live a life worthy of You (Colossians 1:10).
- Strengthen this person with power so that he may have endurance and patience (Colossians 1:11).
- Help this person's love abound more and more in knowledge and depth of insight (Philippians 1:9).

> *Conversing with God becomes part of the rhythm of our lives, a backdrop to all activity, so that our heart becomes our private chapel. The thought,* I can't stand this sermon, *becomes the prayer,* Touch these lives. *To think of someone can be a holy event.*

Our growing intimacy with God can crowd out the negative self-talk, the harping, critical thoughts, the petty criticism —*Good grief! He's wearing polyester pants!* Conversing with God becomes part of the rhythm of our lives, a backdrop to all activity, so that our heart becomes our private chapel. The thought, *I can't stand this sermon*, becomes the prayer, *Touch these lives*. To think of someone can be a holy event.

For example, I felt annoyed each time I looked at the basketball backboard in our yard. My friend's son had pulled the basket down so hard that the backboard broke. He laughed and looked at my son and said, "I guess it's not the kind that pops up."

I felt angry at this boy. We didn't play basketball that much, but when we did we enjoyed it. I hadn't found time to fix the backboard, so every time I looked at it, I felt annoyed with him. I was holding on to my anger, and I knew I needed to surrender it, but how? Uhm. Could the backboard become a reminder to pray for him just as it had been a reminder of being annoyed with him? Just as I was figuring this out, this boy entered a drug rehabilitation center. My fondness for him grew each time I glanced at the backboard and prayed for him.

AUTOMATIC RESPONSES

Those farther down the road than I assure me that being aware of God's presence gradually becomes automatic. The apostle Paul seemed to move in and out of prayer so much that his epistles are an "attractive mixture of prayer, teaching and thanksgiving."[3] Without warning, Paul moves into a prayer: "I ask you, therefore, not to be discouraged because of my sufferings for you, which are your glory. For this reason I kneel before the Father. . . . I pray that out of his glorious riches he may strengthen you" (Ephesians 3:13-16).

Anytime we think about someone, we can turn our hearts toward God. Here are some examples:

- Writing a complimentary close to a letter with the words "Grace and peace to you," reminds us to pray for grace and peace for the recipient of the letter. A closing of "Your friend" becomes a prayer that you can indeed be a friend to this person.
- Participating in a conversation about the failures in our school system is impetus to pray for the local school-board member who riles you or the teachers of children you know.
- Seeing someone's photograph is a reminder to pray for that person, even anonymous photos such as those of missing children on milk cartons.
- Seeing someone who looks like someone you know

becomes an occasion to pray for the person you've recalled.

■ Writing a check to the gas company or a music teacher becomes a prayer asking for wisdom for the recipient.

As we become accustomed to sharing our lives with God in this way, God permeates even these insignificant moments. Martin Luther knew this, for he wrote, "The sigh of a true Christian is a prayer."[4] Perhaps a sigh is the shortest breath prayer of all.

QUESTIONS TO PONDER, EXPERIMENTS TO CONSIDER

Consider asking God to show you what breath prayers you may already use. What favorite Scripture verses could you turn into breath prayers?

———

What events or people in your life do you think of but have never prayed for (committee meetings, coworkers, government or school officials)?

Talking to You
Means Praying for You

I told the pastor I'd be glad to pass out brochures door to door,
but as he handed them to me I thought, *I'd love to go home,
curl up, and read a book.* All my introvertish, shy tendencies oozed
forth. But because I'd agreed to pass out the material, I grit-
ted my teeth and ventured up the walk to the first house.

When a young mother appeared at the door hoisting a tod-
dler on her hip, I unconsciously prayed for her. Seeing the
weary mom triggered it, I'm sure, because I felt like such a mis-
fit mother when my children were small.

I showed her the brochure with the worship service times.
Give her patience, God. This little one isn't potty trained, I prayed.
When I handed her the bright orange pen with the church's
name on it, she smiled. *What a glowing smile — make Yourself real
to her.* As I left the house, I saw that even though my official
task was to pass out literature and pens, my real task was to
bring God's presence to everyone I met.

I enjoyed this new role as pray-er so much that I stopped
at homes on my route abandoned after the Northridge earthquake and prayed for the people who had once lived there.
Living with relatives can be wonderful and difficult, God. Help them

get along. This task of going door to door, which started out as a dreaded duty, became a fun and interesting mission of prayer.

As God becomes our life companion, it seems normal to invite Him to participate in our conversations with others. Frank Laubach described these experiences as "continuous silent conversation of heart to heart with God while looking into other eyes and listening to other voices."[1] You might think this sounds like a confusing dual conversation, but it isn't. Being aware of God's presence helps us focus on the other person so deeply that it's nearly impossible to avoid praying for him or her. We aren't offering long-winded prayers, but "holding forth" a person before God. It's not so much a thought process as a focusing of the heart— an intensity in the gut that enfolds the other person with the love of God. Soon it becomes automatic, "making every glance at another a gentle pressure of prayer."[2]

> *Being aware of God's presence helps us focus on the other person so deeply that it's nearly impossible to avoid praying for him or her.*

SHOW ME THE HEART OF THIS PERSON

Jesus had a way of responding to people that met their deepest needs. With the repentant, He was merciful about their errors; with the self-righteous, He was blunt about them. His secret was that He could read people's hearts (Luke 5:22), which encourages us to pray during conversations: *Show me this person's heart.*

As people's motives and feelings unfold, we may see that God is working within them in ways that surprise us. If we take seriously our role to "consider how we may spur one another on toward love and good deeds" (Hebrews 10:24), we ask God, *How can I be present for them? Is there something they need that I have to offer? How can I cooperate with You, God, in helping them pursue Your purposes for their life?*

When I pray, *Show me these kids' hearts,* as I look into the faces of my two normal yet stubborn teenagers, I am better equipped to pick up their body language and speech cues.

30

Comments their friends or teachers make come to mind. My empathy for them increases and I resist the temptation to think, *Who asked for such stubborn kids?*

Setting aside our expectations and pondering how God is working in someone changes our work and leisure agendas. A troubled coworker is a person to pray for, not just an obstacle to meeting each day's work goal. Sometimes we find, if we're honest, that we don't want to look at the other person's heart because we've been using that person for our own purposes. I experienced this when a particularly fun-loving person I'd spent time with at a conference came to town and asked me to meet her for lunch. Driving to the restaurant, I recalled the hilarious things she said and looked forward to enjoying myself. As we were seated, I sat wide-eyed, waiting for the fun to begin.

Instead, she asked me questions: Why do other Christians seem to love God but I don't? Why do other Christian couples get along but my husband and I struggle so much? Why does God seem out to get me?

I've talked with people many times about these questions, but that day in a sunny restaurant booth sitting with one of the funniest people I know, these questions disappointed and overwhelmed me. The truth was that I didn't want to meet her needs. My mind went blank until I could muster the prayer, *Forgive me, O God.* As I listened, I began asking God, *Help me want to see the heart of this person!* Through this inner conversation with God, I managed to switch gears and set aside the small resentment I felt at missing out on one of those laugh-till-you-cry moments in friendship.

Finally, I made this request of God, *Bring forth what You have put within me.* I'd been told for years I was an encourager, but that day in the restaurant I couldn't imagine how to begin. *Remind me of what You have taught me.* Oh yeah, I'm good at asking questions. So I began asking them. *Show us the obstacles in her way, O God. Make Yourself real to her.* No longer resentful, I felt honored that a friend could be so honest with me.

31

LETTING GOD WORK THE MIRACLES

The first time I knowingly prayed for people at the same time I was talking to them came at my front door while facing two Jehovah's Witnesses. A Christian in a cult-exit ministry had explained to me the crucial truths to present to Jehovah's Witnesses, and I had been faithfully doing this for several years — even to the point of presenting back copies of the *Watchtower*, the publication distributed by their organization, with various discrepancies marked.

> *Perhaps our greatest contribution to any conversation is not what we say, but who we are as we bring Christ's presence with us.*

But my visitors had been instructed by their leaders not to look at such things, so I'd begun to wonder if these conversations were doing any good. As I stood there that day, I decided that the only thing left to do was to pray for them. But what would I pray?

My ex-JW acquaintance had told me that even when he was convinced intellectually that he should leave the cult, he didn't because he was afraid of losing his family and friends. So I prayed as I talked with my visitors: *truth . . . courage . . . assurance . . . love of Christ be with you.* I don't know if they sensed truth or courage, but I sensed that I had brought God's presence to them. I had taken one more step away from performance Christianity. Instead of dazzling my visitors with words, I could bathe them in prayer.

As I described the scene to a friend, I said, "All I could do was pray."

"It's come to that?!" she quipped. "No fancy explanations? No infallible proofs?"

Her teasing reminded me of Oswald Chambers' words: "Prayer does not equip us for greater works — prayer is the greater work."[3] Perhaps our greatest contribution to any conversation is not what we say, but who we are as we bring Christ's presence with us.

IT TAKES PRACTICE

If you should decide to do this and then forget to even try—take heart. In his book *Freedom of Simplicity,* Richard Foster wrote about his attempts to interact with God during conversations for one day:

> One night I made a high resolve: every person whom I saw the next day I would consciously try to lift into the light of Christ. In the morning I jumped up, had breakfast, and was on my way to work before I realized I had not prayed at all for the family. One by one I sought to immerse them in the Light. Once at the office I rushed in, gave the day's work to my secretary, and was walking out the door before I realized my omission once again. I prayed for the joy of the Lord to enter her day. By now I was beginning to realize how far my life was from constant communion. I became *more collected within.* Then as I went through the routine of my day I sought to beam prayers at each one I met. I asked for discernment to perceive what was in people, invited Christ to comfort those who seemed hurt, encourage those who seemed weary, challenge those who seemed indifferent. It was a wonderfully happy day. Sometimes people I would pass on the street would turn, smile and wish me a good day.[4]

If you've worked hard to say and do the right thing, as I have, you too may be stunned at the importance of "being." Our word-hungry, answer-seeking world craves more information, but we can help provide what it *needs*—an awareness of a God who satisfies needs.

QUESTIONS TO PONDER,
EXPERIMENTS TO CONSIDER

What would be a good breath prayer to offer when someone makes a comment or tells a joke you don't like?

Think of someone you admire. What breath prayer could you offer in your conversations with that person?

Wanting to see the heart of people can be difficult. Try substituting the name of someone whose heart is difficult for you to see in the blanks below and offer this prayer, which is used daily by Mother Teresa and the workers at the Calcutta orphanage.

> Dearest Lord, may I see you today and every day in the person of . . . , and, whilst being with them, minister unto you.
>
> Though you hide yourself behind the unattractive disguise of the irritable, the exacting, the unreasonable, may I still recognize you, and say: "Jesus, how sweet it is to serve you."
>
> Lord, give me this seeing faith, then my work will never be monotonous. I will ever find joy in humoring the fancies and gratifying the wishes of all your poor children.
>
> O beloved . . . , how doubly dear you are to me, when you personify Christ; and what a privilege is mine to be allowed to tend you.
>
> Sweetest Lord, make me appreciative of the dignity of my high vocation, and its many responsibilities. Never permit me to disgrace it by giving way to coldness, unkindness, or impatience.
>
> And, O God, while . . . is Jesus, deign also to be a patient Jesus, bearing with my faults, looking only to my intention, which is to love and serve you in the person of each one of these people.
>
> Lord, increase my faith, bless my efforts and work, now and forevermore, Amen.[5]

5

Weaving Prayer with Activity

I could find only eleven business telephone bills for the year—where was the twelfth? I could save a considerable amount in taxes if only I could find that bill! I'm careful with my paperwork for my business, but every year I seem to lose one thing—okay, two or three things.

I prayed, *I know, God, I'm getting upset. This isn't a crisis.*

I've looked in last year's files—I've looked in this year's files. The bill vanished. In what miserable, obscure place could I have put it?

Yes, God, I'm beating up on myself. I know this is wrong. Help me stop.

Back and forth I battle with myself when I figure our income tax. I go from the despair of losing documents to the ecstasy of saving a few dollars. At the end of the day, I'm exhausted. A few years ago, I realized something else as well. I missed God that day. Sure, I bellowed out a breath prayer now and then, but I missed God's abiding presence, something I'd learned to enjoy.

That was when I noticed the candle in the middle of the dining room table where I worked. I resolved that the next year

I would light that candle to remind me to recall God's presence as I work.

And so it's been the last few years. Throughout the roller-coaster emotions of that day, I see in my peripheral vision that candle burning and I mumble, "yes" and "thank You" (that I have an income). The day doesn't sail by smoothly, but that's not the point. I don't keep company with God to guarantee myself a happy life. I do it because I need God, because "I want to know Christ and the power of his resurrection" (Philippians 3:10). Even on such a day, I can enjoy God's presence. I walk through self-flagellation and self-exaltation with a little more grace.

> Our conversations and actions can become holy ground in the sense that the burning bush was for Moses—as a place of conversation with God.

The more we welcome God into our thoughts and conversations, the more we desire His presence everywhere—even in strenuous mental or physical activity. We alternate between focusing on God and focusing on a task until they blend together.[1] Our conversations and actions can become holy ground in the sense that the burning bush was for Moses—as a place of conversation with God.

Prayer can easily be woven into some types of work. The apostle Paul wrote to the Roman Christians, "How constantly I remember you in my prayers *at all times*" (Romans 1:9-10, emphasis added), and we can imagine him doing the hard work of sewing tents to a rhythm of recalling people he had met on his journeys. In my work as a journalist, I picture myself as a "craftsman at his side, filled with delight day after day, rejoicing always in his presence" (Proverbs 8:30).

MUNDANE TASKS

Normal, ordinary activities can seem pointless compared to loftier tasks, but when they're infused with God's presence, they change. The task's wider purpose becomes apparent: I'm not just wiping up a mess in the kitchen, I'm fulfilling my calling as a parent to create a home that provides order in the midst of chaos. Jesus converted a simple act of hygiene, a preparatory act before a meal—the washing of feet—into service to others and worship of God. What an ideal time to pray for someone—on your knees tending that person's feet.

Sometimes it's easier to pray when your body is active and you're comfortable at home. Pat Clary, president and founder of The Women's Ministries Institute, talked to me about how she began to feel overwhelmed in the midst of preparing for the annual Women's Ministry Symposium. Her husband was running for political office, and she had just learned of her mother's terminal illness. Pat felt the need to run away to God. "I closed the office, went home, put on jeans and a sweatshirt and got out my cleaning supplies," she says. "As I was mopping my atrium floor, I began singing hymns to God—some at the top of my voice, others in a quiet lullaby. In the down-to-earth dailiness of life, in my home, I connect best with God, basking in His presence."

Busywork—formatting computer disks, mowing the lawn, cleaning the carpet—invites another level of thinking in which we contemplate the words, wisdom, and challenges of others. This is meditation in its largest sense—pondering the will of God, savoring the ideas of God so that we fulfill the mysterious command to do and say everything in the name of the Lord (Colossians 3:17). Those who choose this contemplative approach to the dailiness of life often find their thoughts converging as they realize that a comment on the telephone five minutes ago provides an answer to the question they asked God earlier in the day. By respecting the rhythm of prayer and work, we create moments for the still, small voice of God to become clear.

As you might suspect, Brother Lawrence prayed within the mundane activities of life:

> I put my little egg-cake into the frying-pan for the love of God. When it is done, and if I have nothing else to call me, I prostrate myself on the ground, and I adore

my God who assists me in everything by His grace; after which I rise up more contented than a king. When I can do nothing else, it is enough for me to lift up a straw for the love of God.[2]

Javonda Barnes, a missionary who spent time at home caring for kids, found reminders throughout the rhythm of her day. As she prepared breakfast, she prayed

> *By respecting the rhythm of prayer and work, we create moments for the still, small voice of God to become clear.*

for people in Russia whose daily food was not a certainty. As her children got ready for school, she sensed God's prompting to pray for their teachers and administrators and other school personnel, for her friends who were mothers and their children's school-day needs. In the grocery line, she prayed for people whose names filled the tabloid headlines. On walks with her children, she prayed for teenagers she passed whom she felt might be tempted.[3]

Singing is also an ideal way to relate to God because it's such a whole-being activity. The mind remembers the words, the emotions follow the melody, and the body inhales and exhales the rhythm of the prayer. When a friend's husband felt depressed and confused in career transition, I found myself rehearsing a line from a worship song about God making the weak strong. When a top-forty song about abstinence became popular, I prayed it as my daughter listened to it on the car radio.

REMINDERS THAT BRING US HOME

Events in your life probably already lend themselves to prayer, but you may not realize it. Here are some other ideas for infusing prayer into your everyday activities.

Sense-related reminders. The sound of an ambulance siren, the ringing of a telephone, or a child calling out "Dad" can remind us to pray for the person in need. Others use visual reminders, such as carrying a stone in a pocket, wearing a cross, or taping a phrase of Scripture to the wall of your work area.

I especially need a sense of God's presence when I'm conducting a difficult telephone interview in my work as a journalist. After I saw how well the lit candle worked while figuring my income tax, I lit a candle during interviews, but I forgot about the candle because my senses were focused elsewhere: my eyes on my computer monitor and my ear on the voice on the telephone. So I tried a vanilla-scented candle, and this now-familiar scent wafts from the far end of my desk, reminding me to enjoy God's presence as His much-loved child. In that strength I can move forward even when it seems an interview is going nowhere.

Margins of time. Many of us fast-hoof it through life as if we have to orchestrate life's events with the productivity of an efficiency expert. Instead of flitting from one activity to another, we can build slots of downtime between tasks and schedule appointments a little further apart. Then we can focus on each experience and be receptive to God's presence within it. This deliberate awareness goes against the hurry, hastiness, and greed of a culture that urges us to pack as many useful tasks into a day as possible. These spaces of time make it easier to ask God questions and ponder His ways.

Slowing down the body. Tilden Edwards, director of the Shalem Institute for Spiritual Formation, advises that the way we move corresponds with how conscious we are of God's presence. "Think of the way we move when we are on retreat. Almost certainly we find ourselves slowing down. . . . We are there precisely to release that 'in charge' manner and listen for the real Presence here and now, moment by moment. . . . We need to move evenly, gracefully, aware that every movement of leg, arm and head is centered in God, not outside. . . . A jerked around body encourages a jerky, fragmented mind," which is "outside the One in whom we are called to 'live and *move* and have our being'" (Acts 17:28).[4] I've had to ask God to help me recognize when I'm hunching my shoulders or holding my breath, because I don't realize I'm doing these things. Once we're aware of it, we can surrender the hurry or tension and, secure in God's presence, relax the shoulders and take deep breaths.

WEAVING PRAYER THROUGHOUT OUR TASKS

In his book *Finding God at Home,* hospital chaplain Ernest Boyer, Jr., reflected on Brother Lawrence's recommendations for weaving prayer throughout our tasks and offered these four suggestions, which I have paraphrased:[5]

> *Nothing that we do is too ordinary or too boring for God. He delights in us not because we are entertaining, but because we are His.*

Reflect before beginning each task. Before starting any job, stop for a minute or two and remind yourself that at that moment "you delight God in a thousand and one ways. . . . God loves you just as you are. . . . Try to feel this great love directed toward you, so that when you begin your work you make it a response to that love."

Brother Lawrence said the following prayer before he began anything:

> My God, since You are with me, and since it is Your will that I should apply my mind to these outward things, I pray that You will give me the grace to remain with You and keep company with You. But so that my work may be better, Lord, work with me; receive my work and possess all my affections.[6]

Within days of my placing that quotation on the wall behind my computer monitor at work, a new breath prayer permeated my workday: "Receive my work; possess all my affections."

Repeat a short prayer as you work. Use breath prayers such as, "God loves me," "I delight in You, God," or "This task is for You, God." You may want to come up with a rhythm to your work—changing breath prayers as you plant each seed or wash each dish.

Reflect after you finish each task. Take a minute to enjoy finishing the task and offer it to God.

Turn thoughts and feelings to God as you work. Invite God to join you in the chatter in your head and consider how each wandering thought—a complaint, a question, a memory—can become a prayer.

Nothing that we do is too ordinary or too boring for God. He delights in us not because we are entertaining, but because we are His.

QUESTIONS TO PONDER, EXPERIMENTS TO CONSIDER

What, if anything, sounds too difficult about talking and listening to God while you're doing something else?

————

A Filipino farmer told Laubach, "I used to farm with my hand on the plow, my eyes on the furrow, but my mind on God."[7] If you were to paraphrase these words, how would you change the italicized phrases that follow to fit your lifestyle? I *farm with my hand on the plow, my eyes on the furrow,* but my mind on God.

————

If you were going to pray before beginning a task, which of the following prayers might you say?

- "God loves me."
- "I delight in You, God."
- "This task is for You, God."
- "Receive my work."
- Your own prayer:

6

Praying Without Words

One morning when my daughter, Janae, was in fifth grade, she couldn't find her permission slip for a field trip. She searched her room, which was usually messy even though I— a supermom in those days—had given her guidelines for cleaning it and consequences for when she didn't. I wrote my own permission slip and she left for school upset.

I sank onto the sofa wondering, *Why is this child so unorganized? What more could I do?* I wanted to treasure her, but she frustrated me. I felt angry with myself that I let a messy room upset me so much. I sank deeper into despair: *How can I accept her and accept myself? I love this child and want to have a servant's heart, but how can I show it when her habits drive me nuts?* I had asked God these questions so often that I couldn't bear to pray them one more time.

Then I remembered a story I'd read about a woman who did one small act of kindness each day in secret. This was difficult for her because she lived in a dormitory and her roommates might have caught her. She did this secretly, she wrote, because "it gave me an inner excitement to do this only for God."[1]

Yes, I thought, *I am out of words for prayer, but I can say what I want to say to God (and perhaps to Janae) by doing some small act of kindness instead.* So I ambled into Janae's room and made her bed for her—something I rarely do. First, I cleaned out the books and dolls and purses she had stuffed under her covers. Then with precision and joy, I pulled the sheet and bedspread up and tucked them in with neat hospital-style corners. By the time I arranged her stuffed animals in a circle kissing each other (she'd love that!), I sensed God's grace for me and for her. This was my way of saying to God: *No, I am not a perfect mother and she is not a perfect daughter, but I trust that You will work with us anyway.*

Sometimes words aren't a large enough container to hold the messages we want to express to God. It's easier to communicate with God through a physical activity: digging weeds, rocking a baby, playing the drums, or even making a bed. These actions, in some inexplicable way, become prayers.

This is different from praying while doing an activity, as described in the last chapter. This is when the action itself—no matter how mundane—becomes a wordless prayer. Brother Lawrence was glad to pick up a straw from the ground for no other reason than out of his love for God.[2]

Work, especially, seems to change its flavor when done as part of our pleasure in knowing God. Many of us are lazy by nature and do as little as we can; or we huff and puff at our work, completing the last detail, eager to hear the words, "You're a pro—you always do things well." It's a radical idea to use our work to glorify God, to relish our love for Him. As we do, we pay attention to details for reasons other than seeking self-congratulation: "There is something very beautiful in

> *Sometimes words aren't a large enough container to hold the messages we want to express to God. It's easier to communicate with God through a physical activity: digging weeds, rocking a baby, playing the drums, or even making a bed. These actions, in some inexplicable way, become prayers.*

work which is well and precisely done. It is a participation in the activity of God, who makes all things well and wisely, beautiful to the last detail."[3]

WHEN ACTIONS SPEAK LOUDER THAN WORDS

If we allow our actions to become prayers, we may begin to see our bodies as instruments of praise to God. Much of Western Christianity has embraced the Greek idea of elevating spirit over matter. This idea has God using the mind and will and perhaps emotions but regarding the body as an ill-fitted container, a necessary evil to get our minds from place to place.

Is this a scriptural idea? On the one hand, the body is described as corruptible or perishable (1 Corinthians 15:53, KJV, NIV), and Christ says evil things pour forth from it to defile humankind (Mark 7:20-23). On the other hand, our bodies are "members of Christ" (1 Corinthians 6:15), and the body is "for the Lord, and the Lord for the body" (1 Corinthians 6:13). The body, then, can hinder or help our relationship with God.

In his book *The Spirit of the Disciplines*, philosophy professor and Southern Baptist minister Dallas Willard writes,

> We tend to think of the body and its functions as only
> a hindrance to our spiritual calling, with no positive
> role in our redemption. . . . The spiritual and the bodily
> are by no means opposed in human life—they are
> complementary.[4]

Our bodies can partner in our experience with God when they serve as tools to enhance our relationship with Him. This is illustrated well by biblical figures who worshiped God with their bodies—Paul fasted (Acts 14:23), David danced before the Lord (2 Samuel 6:14-15), Jewish assemblies raised their hands and clapped (Psalm 47:1).

But how does this partnership happen? The body must be retrained, especially in this age where we have been encouraged to use our bodies to achieve goals and chase pleasure.

This retraining is done, Dallas Willard explains, through spiritual disciplines.[5] Just as fasting or chastity retrain the body to focus on God by abstaining from eating and sexual activity, the discipline of practicing God's presence can teach the body to enjoy and worship God in all of life.

The specific ways our bodies participate in enjoying God's presence differ from person to person. Scripture gives us a start by pointing to positions such as kneeling and lying prostate and to movements such as singing, clapping, and lifting hands. While some are appropriate for public worship, others work better in solitude. Alone with God, we can feel free to fall on our faces seeking Him or to twirl in delight that He delivered us from temptation.

> *Our bodies can become partners in our experience with God when they serve as tools to enhance our relationship with Him.*

Bodily "prayers" often weave themselves into daily life. When God's will is done, we pull back the arm and fist with a visceral "Yes!" In moments of conviction, we wordlessly cover our faces with our hands to ask forgiveness and offer surrender. In this way, we "make every part of [our] body into a weapon fighting on the side of God" (Romans 6:13, JB).

If we try to retrain our thoughts without retraining our body, our body may rebel at having been left out. I saw this clearly in my body's response to the distant aftershocks of the 1994 Northridge earthquake. Exactly one year after the quake, an earthquake occurred in Kobe, Japan, and I began having private aftershocks—a not uncommon sensation of feeling an aftershock when none actually occurred. I tried using each aftershock as a reminder to pray for the people in Kobe. That helped my mind, but my body was not stilled for days.

Six months later, a 4.9 aftershock awakened our family in the night just as the original quake had. After calming all the teenagers staying with us that night, I sat on the floor and began to shake violently. I wrapped myself in a blanket, which caused the shaking to stop, but my body would not relax or sleep or focus throughout the night. The next morning I couldn't work, so I began to sing a soothing worship song. Because it was a song to which the little kids in our church swayed, I swayed too. My breathing relaxed first as the singing retrained my lungs to breathe regularly, and then I noticed that my arms relaxed and hung limp at my sides as they often do during our worship service. The swaying provided my trunk and torso a steady reassuring motion of being rocked in God's lap. That's when I realized that my body had to take an active part in the calming process of prayer. I couldn't *think* my body into God's peace.

BENEFITS OF ACTIVE PRAYER

For those of us who have worked so hard to pray the right words that we have no idea what's in our heart, speaking to God through an action is a relief. We follow our instincts. Instead of planning and plotting, we can be spontaneous. We experience a certain wonder and innocence, much like a small child extending her arms up to her dad asking to be held.

An action-prayer can help us say and hear things that can't easily be put into words. For example, runner and missionary Eric Liddell felt God's pleasure when he ran. Others have sensed God's pleasure when they surf or hike or ride their horse. Enjoying God's presence is part of the reason they do these things, although they may rarely say so.

During some of my aerobic exercise sessions, I enjoy God's presence intensely. I have a sense that God is watching me, His small child, as I move my tired and stiff body with grace and energy. My legs and arms move to a rhythm God has placed inside me, even though Jane Fonda appears before me on the television screen. In the midst of all this enjoyment, I get creative ideas for writing, for serving, for loving my family.

These active prayers pull faith into everyday moments, demonstrating that God is not limited to activities such as Bible reading and church attendance. Active prayer wipes out the artificial separation of faith from everyday life and invites God into the cracks and crevices of our existence. Nothing we do is without the company of God. Slowly we come closer to the difficult-to-fathom goal of offering our bodies and everything else we are as a living sacrifice, holy and pleasing to God — this becomes a daily spiritual act of worship (Romans 12:1).

QUESTIONS TO PONDER, EXPERIMENTS TO CONSIDER

What kinds of activities seem like prayers to you?

———

When, if ever, have you had the kind of experience embodied in the following sentence? "Any work done for love is an act of worship. It becomes a special devotion, a prayer."

———

What phrase within the following prayer, if any, expresses your response to this chapter? "God, creator of my body, I've never been sure how to 'glorify God in the body.' Show me how to retrain it to become a vital part of my relationship with You. Help me follow Your leading."

7

Focusing on What's in Front of You

As I drove my teenagers home that night, I was immersed in thoughts of buying a newer house. The homes up the hill from us had interior walls that weren't chipped, cabinets that weren't dated, and grass that was greener. My mind strode back and forth down that street.

Then I caught myself. I was doing the American thing— longing for bigger and better material goods. I knew better than that. We sponsored a child in a Third World country, and I volunteered at a shelter for the homeless. Was it God's will to use the money our family earned to live in an impressive home? Did I think a newer home would satisfy me? No, but when my mind wanders, I sometimes obsess on things that are contrary to who I believe I am.

So then, what shall I turn my thoughts to? *Blank.* Easy answer. I can continue my experiment of enjoying God's presence, but how? I drew another blank. *God, I appreciate Your presence, but . . . blank again.* I looked harder at what was in front of me—only a dark freeway. *God, what can we talk about now?*

Suddenly, I saw the answer everywhere. I was driving past

the off ramp that had collapsed in the Northridge earthquake four months before. The tires of my car were rolling along the portion of the freeway that had been closed for repairs. *O God, help the many people who are still homeless from the earthquake work out the details of where to live. Calm those like me who are stunned by aftershocks. Grant safety to the construction workers who labor in the median a few feet from me.* The prayers went on and on. Each agonizing thought about the earthquake turned into a request for the people around me.

As our lifelong journey of enjoying union with God picks up momentum, we become more intentional about enjoying God's presence. We find simple ways to turn our focus back to God. Missionary Frank Laubach, who recorded his interesting experiments in practicing God's presence, enjoyed playing a "game with minutes," as he called it. He began by "trying to line up my actions with the will of God about every fifteen minutes or every half hour. . . . I have started out trying to live all my waking moments in conscious listening to the inner voice, asking without ceasing, 'What, Father, do you desire said? What, Father, do you desire done this minute?'"[1]

Some have tried Laubach's approach while others have simply adopted its purpose—turning their attention to God as often as they can. That intentional shift of attention drives us to examine the person, place, or thing in front of us and find something in it that leads us into conversation with God. As I gaze at the teenagers and coaches at my son's cross-country meets, I pray, *Give these kids confidence; build patience into these coaches. Is there something I can say or do to help that happen?* The water flowing through the pipes as I brush my teeth in the morning reminds me to pray, *Give strength to families in Third World countries who haul water many times a day.* Watching the store clerk in front of me means praying, *I don't know his needs, but since I need more of You, God, he probably does too.*

In the moments before speaking at retreats, I used to get nervous, hoping that the content I'd prepared would meet needs and that my delivery would make it easy for listeners to hear. Then I remembered my experiment: Pray for whatever is in front of you. So I looked at the retreat attendees and bathed them in prayer. I started mingling in the crowd and talking with people before I spoke, asking God: *Show me my mission here today. Who at this gathering do You want me to talk to? To listen to? To laugh with? To reach with my words?* Without trying to relax, I did.

WHOLE-LIFE PRAYER

In my many journeys through the book *A Diary of Private Prayer*, I've been struck by how author John Baillie prayed for advancements in science, education, and true learning[2] and praised God for music and books and good company and "all pure pleasures."[3] Even though I believed that nothing in this world was out of bounds for prayer, I had somehow eliminated certain topics as too ordinary or too much a part of "real life" (as opposed to my sheltered Christian world?) to pray about. So I started praying for leaders in fields I cared a lot about: art, education, and religion. As I pondered this, I prayed for the first time for:

- curators of art museums; influential contemporary authors such as John Irving and Pat Conroy; powerful movie producers, such as Steven Spielberg;
- the state superintendent of schools; professors in schools of education; and
- leaders of Islam, Buddhism, and Hinduism.

This last group stunned me most of all. How could I have studied about and taught classes on major world religions but never prayed that the leaders of those religions would come to know the truth about God? I could sense my role in life expanding from learning and teaching to include watching and praying.

But why restrict my prayer to leaders in these fields? Isn't God's heart for the downtrodden and despised? In the same categories as above, I began praying for:

- new artists who are held suspect by art reviewers;
- struggling students who don't seem to fit into any educational system; and
- those who are burned out with church and can't find their way back.

Praying for whatever is in front of us includes praying while reading the newspaper or watching the news. Wars around the world aren't just news, they're calls to pray for God's will to be done, for justice to prevail. When reading political cartoonists and outstanding editorial writers, we can pray they'll become instruments of truth and peace—whether or not they're aware of it.

Practicing God's presence this way, then, is not an escape from the world but an engagement of the world. We process the tragedy and viciousness through our awareness that God is active in every situation. In so doing, we find one more way of fulfilling the commission Christ gave us to interact with a world that cries out for redemption in the midst of chaos.

LIVING CONSCIOUSLY

While it's futile to strain to enjoy God's presence, we must be intentional about it. As seekers, we become deliberate and aware. We pay attention to God's unfolding presence in every situation: What is God saying? What is His will here? Then without trying, a thought about how bright the sunlight is today becomes a smile of gratitude to God for creating such light.

This involves training the eye to see and trusting that it will find something to appreciate. The more we train

> *While it's futile to strain to enjoy God's presence, we must be intentional about it. As seekers, we become deliberate and aware. We pay attention to God's unfolding presence in every situation: What is God saying? What is His will here? Then without trying, a thought about how bright the sunlight is today becomes a smile of gratitude to God for creating such light.*

51

ourselves to see, the more we see. In *Pilgrim at Tinker Creek*, Annie Dillard wrote, "I have just learned to see praying mantis egg cases. Suddenly I see them everywhere."[4] It's the same in the spiritual life—we grow in our sense of God's presence. We become attentive to how God works. Deliberately mentioning what we see to God helps us build these seeing skills. "Seeing is of course very much a matter of verbalization. Unless I call my attention to what passes before my eyes, I simply won't see it."[5] In this way we learn the art of attentiveness, of leaning into the situation or relationship with alert eyes.

YET THE MIND WANDERS . . .

Laubach predicted as much: "Mind wandering must be endured by all who would learn this discipline. . . . But we need not feel discouraged when we fail. . . . After months and years of practicing the presence of God, one feels that God is closer; His push from behind seems to be stronger and steadier, and the pull from in front seems to grow strong."[6]

When my mind wanders, I like to let my prayers follow it. *Uhm, so I'm thinking of my husband's coworker—where is God in that? Is He saying something? Should I inquire about that coworker?* Following the wandering mind with our prayers can be an adventure. Prayer takes on a life of its own as we move from topic to topic, from praise to admitting mistakes, from thanks to requests. The ebb and flow resembles that remarkable communication between individuals called conversation.

We let God forgive our wandering mind, expressed so honestly in this prayer:

Why, O Lord, is it so hard for me to keep my heart directed toward you? Why do the many little things I want to do, and the many people I know, keep crowding into my mind, even during the hours I am totally free to be with you and you alone? Why does my mind wander off in so many directions, and why does my heart desire the things that lead me astray? Are you not enough for me? Do I keep doubting your love and care, your mercy and grace? Do I keep wondering, in the center of my being, whether you will give me all I need if I just keep my eyes on you?

Please accept my distractions, my fatigue, my irritations, and my faithless wanderings. You know me more deeply and fully than I know myself. You love me with a greater love than I can love myself. You even offer me more than I can desire. Look at me, see me in all my misery and inner confusion, and let me sense your presence in the midst of my turmoil. All I can do is show myself to you. Yet, I am afraid to do so. I am afraid that you will reject me. But I know—with the knowledge of faith—you desire to give me your love. The only thing you ask of me is not to hide from you, not to run away in despair, not to act as if you were a relentless despot.

Take my tired body, my confused mind, and my restless soul into your arms and give me rest, simple quiet rest. Do I ask too much too soon? I should not worry about that. You will let me know. Come, Lord Jesus, come. Amen.[7]

QUESTIONS TO PONDER, EXPERIMENTS TO CONSIDER

What is in front of you at this moment that provides a topic of conversation with God?

————

Which leaders in fields you care about (art, education, religion, music, technology, sports) would you like to pray for?

————

Pick out a few lines from the above prayer that express what you have wanted to say to God, but haven't.

Finding God in Irritating Moments

Each week it got worse. As I traveled back and forth to work in a car pool, I thought I would explode. It seemed to me that one of my coworkers and car-pool companions complained nonstop. I tried to pray for her, but I am not the saint I would like to be. At traffic signals, I wanted to bolt from the van and run.

I considered that she was emotionally needy and I admitted to God that I could not make her okay—nor was I willing to try. When I prayed for her, I imagined her sitting in God's lap, which is an image I often use for myself when I feel needy. This helped for a while, but by the next week, I still wanted to flee the van.

While digging around in our storage shed, I discovered a child-size rocking chair that had been my daughter's. I tilted it and watched it rock. A spontaneous prayer for my coworker occurred somewhere within me. *Hhhm, interesting.* I dragged the rocking chair into my kitchen and placed it in a corner. It was in the way and didn't fit my kitchen's contemporary look, but it helped. Each time I walked by it, I tilted it and offered a breath prayer for my coworker. I can't report that I became instantly patient with her, because I didn't. But the resentment was gone, and I guessed that God was pleased with that much obedience. And more of my life was filled with an awareness of God's companionship.

So much for anyone who thinks that enjoying God's presence is only for mild-mannered, angel-faced mystics. Even those of us who will never be even-tempered, easygoing saints can enjoy this discipline. If you're miles away from "loving your enemies," you might be able to muster up a breath prayer for them (Matthew 5:44-45). That irritating neighbor's uncut grass or the unfamiliar car parked in your apartment's parking space becomes a signal to mumble, *Turn this person's heart toward You* or *What is it You want to show me through this person?*

Besides these SOS prayers, we can converse with God about irritations in a manner much like Tevya, the distraught father of three daughters in *Fiddler on the Roof.* His way of throwing his hands in the air, searching upward and asking God outrageous questions makes the audience laugh, perhaps more out of envy than dismay. Tevya is not out of line. His searching spirit resembles that of Habakkuk, the prophet of Judah who stood on the ramparts and posed questions to God.

Tevya, Habakkuk, and the psalmists remind us that there is room for passion in our life with God. For too long, the passion in the Gospels has been ignored. I've tried to picture Jesus saying, "You brood of vipers!" with a calm, detached look on His face, and it doesn't ring true. Just as Christ became frustrated by the sin around Him, we can expect to be frustrated too. Because the angry, passionate psalms are overlooked, we forget how the psalmists often made outrageous accusations in their cries for help. My favorite is:

Those who hate me without reason
    outnumber the hairs of my head. (Psalm 69:4)

Did the psalmist really have an endless number of enemies, or did it just feel that way? Like Tevya, we can confess our confusion and perplexity — throwing up dust, asking questions, declaring, "I don't get it!"

Some of us seem afraid to tell God about the anger and frustration that He already knows we feel. Or we deny feeling anger because we assume that God and anger cannot coexist. Instead, we put on a "looking good, kid" image with God— we look good, we feel good, we are good. Anger and frustration are regarded as obstacles to be overcome and replaced with worthy feelings—before we talk to God.

CONFESSING TO GOD WHO WE ARE

To abide in God's presence means that we don't have to dress up our feelings. If we believe God is grand enough to love our flawed self, we can speak the truth to Him about what we feel—anger at others, disappointment with ourselves, resentment toward Him, the Creator. God's presence can be a safe place to reveal our laziness, our grouchiness, and our self-congratulatory ways. God invites transparent confessions about how we pretend to be better than we are, how we avoid serving when it's inconvenient, how we care for our friends best when they make us feel good, and how we focus our energy and efforts on acquiring things—just the right belt, the right stereo, the right computer chip. Confession is important not because God needs this information but because we need to be willing to give it. In this way, our conversation with God becomes open, honest, and personal.

> *To abide in God's presence means that we don't have to dress up our feelings. If we believe God is grand enough to love our flawed self, we can speak the truth to Him about what we feel—anger at others, disappointment with ourselves, resentment toward Him, the Creator.*

Consider the famous conversations between God and those who obeyed Him. Moses is often criticized for making excuses that he couldn't talk in front of others (Exodus 3–4), yet anyone who has ever had stage fright can feel relieved to link up with a God who offers confidence to a fearful Moses. In

Gideon's conversation with the angel of the Lord, God performed fleece tricks to provide reassurance to this non-hero who dared to talk back to an angel (Judges 6:15,36). When Mary asked the puzzling scientific question, "How can this be . . . ?" (Luke 1:34, RSV), Gabriel was not impatient with her. God was not upset or offended by these expressions of doubt and frustration.

"What is true in our human friendships is also true in friendship with God with respect to our prayer," writes Roberta Bondi, professor of church history at Candler School of Theology. She continues:

> It is imperative that we speak our true minds to God. That means that when we pray we do not worry about the suitability of our prayer. We do not concern ourselves with wondering if what we are praying for is unworthy of God's attention, and we do not worry about being respectful. We tell God what we carry in our hearts, and we ask God what we need for ourselves and for others, not to make ourselves feel better but because our friendship with God needs it.[1]

WON'T WE TRY GOD'S PATIENCE?

Sure, God was patient with Moses, Gideon, and Mary when they asked, Who am I, that I should . . . ? How do I know? How can this be?—but we don't feel comfortable asking those questions. Where does God draw the line?

To ask questions is not the same as to disobey. Refusing to obey means walking away from God's will, as Jonah did (Jonah 1:3). Sometimes we, like Jonah, don't ask a question or say a word, but quietly refuse to do what God asks. It's wiser to offer God our passionate questions so He can help us obey. Then we're engaging and seeking God even though we're confused, scared, or angry. Our searching nurtures the passion that keeps us looking at God, talking with God, and listening to God.

But won't God get angry? God's anger did burn against

Moses when he finally pleaded, "Please send someone else" (Exodus 4:13), but even then God didn't act in anger. He acted in great love, designating Aaron as a companion to Moses. To what does God respond in anger? The most consistent example is His punishment of Israel. God punished them when they rebelled against Him by idolizing their life in Egypt (Numbers 16) and by worshiping idols. God's wrath is against disobedience and unrighteousness (Romans 1:18). Offering God our irritations is not unrighteousness, but a way to keep ourselves from unrighteousness. It helps us avoid outward rage and prolonged bitterness as we attempt, day by day, to turn over unruly feelings and inappropriate desires to God.

It's as if we're afraid of upsetting God. Yet the psalmists fumed about their fear and anger in the imprecatory psalms (these include such Psalms as 58, 69, 109, 129, 137, 140). Here are a few lines from one of David's:

> Break the teeth in their mouths, O God;
>   tear out, O Lord, the fangs of the lions!
> Let them vanish like water that flows away;
>   when they draw the bow, let their arrows be blunted.
> Like a slug melting away as it moves along,
>   like a stillborn child, may they not see the sun.
> Before your pots can feel the heat of the thorns—
>   whether they be green or dry—
> the wicked will be swept away. (Psalm 58:6-9)

How can these prayers be a part of the Bible when we're told to be peacemakers? Perhaps they tell us that the way to move from anger to peacemaking is to go *through* the anger, not to deny it. Praying as the psalmists did is about "pouring out our souls" to God (Psalm 42:4). They give us permission to unload on God instead of unleashing anger and vengeance on others. Within this process of gathering our anger into words and presenting it to God, we are often powerfully convicted of sin. Hearing these words ring in the air, we find the contrition to say, *God, forgive me for this anger. Show me the way forward. Do not abandon me to my rage.*

These psalms then become a model of unleashing our anger not in prayers of vengeance but in prayers of release. This helps us follow the command to resolve anger before the sun sets (Ephesians 4:26), so that our anger does not ferment into bitterness.

None of this is to say that God becomes our little buddy at whom we yammer. To have the "fear of the Lord" is a wise thing—it would be foolish not to fear God, so full of holiness, power, and majesty as He is. A healthy, active fear of God does not paralyze us, however. God will not strike us dead if we show anger; He is not insulted by our humanness.

In order to abide in Christ and enjoy God's presence, we must learn not to pretend to be okay. Withholding our true feelings blocks the development of an intimate relationship with God. Notice how Mary and Martha did not shrink from speaking their minds to Jesus: "If you had been here, my brother would not have died" (John 11:21,32). Only Martha, but not Mary, added the hopeful statement, "But I know that even now God will give you whatever you ask" (John 11:22). Mary and Martha were rigorously honest about their feelings. Did their honesty irritate Jesus? The text doesn't say, so we don't know. But He didn't reject them or try to "whip them into shape" with a sermon. After comforting them with words of truth about the resurrection, Jesus went to the tomb and wept publicly, revealing His feelings of grief.

> In the shelter of such a friendship, we can tell God what we really think. We don't have to hide from Him when we're angry. We can grumble, we can spit out our breath prayers, we can go into our closets and scream.

In the shelter of such a friendship, we can tell God what we really think. We don't have to hide from Him when we're angry. We can grumble, we can spit out our breath prayers, we can go into our closets and scream.

At times, our conversation with God may imitate the way Samuel's mother, Hannah, poured out her soul to God because of her infertility. She was so intense that the priest Eli assumed she was drunk (1 Samuel 1:14)! Or we may call a timeout from life for a psalm-session that follows the psalmists' frequent pattern of making outrageous statements, gradually recounting God's past deliverance, and ending in praise or pleas that God intervene.

From that psalm-session, we can form a breath prayer or keep a symbol (a rocking chair, a lit candle) nearby to remind us of God's continual attention to our irritation. In this way, prayer moves from an act of obedience to a point of relief, and in so doing, cements our friendship with God.

QUESTIONS TO PONDER, EXPERIMENTS TO CONSIDER

Think of an irritating person in your life. What does that person need? What common object in your house or workplace could you use to remind you to pray for that person's need to be met?

———

What prayers, thoughts, or feelings have you hidden from God?

———

In what ways can you see practicing the presence of God as a help in working through the irritations of life?

Loving God
in Anguished Moments

When I entered the darkness of the church's auditorium, I wasn't sure why I had come. My kids were attending youth group several buildings away, and I felt drawn to sit there as I pondered my anguish over several friends at church. Thinking about one of them, a man with a terminal disease, I sat in his usual chair on the right side of the auditorium. There in the darkness I tried to pray for him, but words would not come. So I sat there and grieved for him. I found myself hunched over, elbows on my knees, head in my hands—just as he always sat. I knew I was praying for him, but I couldn't tell you what I said.

After a few minutes, I moved across the room to the seat where another friend usually sat. She felt betrayed by another church member and was crumbling inside, but didn't want anyone to know it. I sat upright and tall in her chair, as she always did. She often wore a look on her face that said, "I'm going forth! Watch out!" and so did I as I sat in wordless prayer for her.

Finally, I moved toward the center aisle and slid into the seat of a friend who was separated from his wife. He always extended his arm across the empty chair next to him as if he were waiting for her to sit there, and I did the same. As I felt his grief, it became clear to me that each of them felt rejected by God in some way. My prayer found these words: "Help them know You love them."

It was then I realized that it wasn't smart to sit alone in a dark building in a gangland neighborhood. What had driven me to sit there? I had prayed so much for these friends for weeks that a little prayer sprinkled here and there was no longer enough. The time had come to agonize in the dark for them, to focus on them in a determined way.

After a while I left to run some errands, and when I went to pick up my kids, I saw the lights on in the auditorium. I tiptoed in, and there sat one of the men I had prayed for, playing the piano. I hesitated, then walked toward him, leaned over, and said, "You are loved desperately by God." His face looked blank, but his eyes filled. "That's exactly what I need to hear," he said.

When anguish is too deep for words, it helps to sit in it as Job sat in the ashes (Job 2:8). This is contrary to the popular image of a Christian: a victorious overcomer who is always fine and never frustrated. Circumstances never puzzle these super saints; people never bewilder them. For them, it seems as if God banishes pain and perplexity from life.

Scripture, of course, teaches otherwise. David writes,

> The Lord is close to the brokenhearted
>   and saves those who are crushed in spirit.
>   (Psalm 34:18)

And the apostle Paul was perplexed even as he did God's will: "We are hard pressed on every side, but not crushed; *perplexed*, but not in despair; persecuted, but not abandoned; struck down, but not destroyed" (2 Corinthians 4:8-9, emphasis added).

Times of anguish can transform us if we push away self-pity and put our energy into longing for God. In moments of brokenness, we can almost taste and touch the psalmist's yearning:

As the deer pants for streams of water,
  so my soul pants for you, O God.
My soul thirsts for God, for the living God.
  When can I go and meet with God? (Psalm 42:1-2)

When troubled circumstances end, the yearning stays and we continue to savor God's presence. A strong friendship has been built and we don't want to let go. Throughout Abraham's waiting periods and perplexing life episodes, he "'believed God, and it was credited to him as righteousness,' and he was called God's friend" (James 2:23).

GOD'S PRESENCE IN PAIN

Those who see God as all sweetness and light are tempted to run from Him in painful moments. But in our pain, we are to cry out to God:

As a woman with child and about to give birth
  writhes and cries out in her pain,
    so were we in your presence, O LORD. (Isaiah 26:17,
      emphasis added)

During the Los Angeles riots, I suffered great pain as I watched the neighborhood that had been my home for many years burn. I cringed at the disparaging remarks of my new suburban neighbors who acted as if every south-central Los Angeles resident were a looter. My former neighbors were people of great courage, and I admired them. I didn't realize how continuously I was praying for them until my husband chuckled at what he called my "Gethsemane pose" over the newspaper. Unconsciously I had extended my arms and hands in front of me, as Jesus is often pictured in Gethsemane. I grieved for the families of the victims as I read their names in the newspaper. I pondered what I needed to cancel in order to participate in the cleanup that Saturday. I begged God to lead Christians to show more grace and mercy.

GOD'S PRESENCE IN TEMPTATION

Perhaps the moments when God's presence is most unwanted or scary is during temptation. Who wants to talk to God, much less enjoy His presence, when they're about to eat two submarine sandwiches or trash someone's reputation? But practicing God's presence during temptation is part of what it means to "stand firm"(Ephesians 6:14). In the novel *Glittering Images*, fictional clergyman Charles Ashworth exuded this firm stance when, after making a suggestive remark to a woman friend, he promptly elevated the tone of the conversation. The woman noticed the shift and commented, "God's at the centre of your life, isn't He? He doesn't just fade away when things are going well, as He does with most people. He's there all the time— and . . . you *know* He's there."[1]

> To rest in God's companionship in the midst of temptation provides a lifeline of strength.

To rest in God's companionship in the midst of temptation provides a lifeline of strength. As an acquaintance and I were complaining about a company we had both worked for, he stopped in mid-sentence and said, "God's yanking my chain. I don't need to talk this way. They did their best and I appreciate it." His mid-sentence repentance modeled for me the importance of listening to God's nudges and responding to them as soon as I'm able.

Sometimes, temptation is so invasive that it seems to crowd out God's presence. While wrestling with a tough temptation once, I felt the need to physically escape into a place I reserve for enjoying God's presence. Armed with my walking shoes and worship tape, I spent hours walking a nearby canyon road, crying out to God. I picked up wads of sagebrush and tossed them over the steep bank of the creek to show my resolve. "I'm sick of being so weak. I want out," I yelled. "This is crowding You out of my life, God. I want You back."

A week later, on the canyon road again, I stamped my foot and said, "When will You take away this problem, God? When will

64

I give it up? Tell me what to do." As you can guess, nothing happened. So I kept walking. As I stared at the canyon walls, I thought of my son who skillfully rappels down the sides of cliffs. *That's not me,* I thought. *I'm scared, I'm weak. I'd never rappel. I'd be clinging to the sides of the cliffs.*

Cling? Didn't the psalmist *cling*? The line of the worship song resonated within me: "You have been my help in time of need. Lord, unto You will I cling." I saw that my error had been in trying to perform stunts for God, trying to be a temptation-proof Christian. I could stand firm against temptation only by clinging to God as I would to the side of a cliff. Here's how the psalmist put it:

> Because you are my help,
>   I sing in the shadow of your wings.
> My soul *clings* to you;
>   your right hand upholds me. (Psalm 63:7-8,
>   emphasis added)

STRENGTH FROM WEAKNESS

In these distressing moments, we lay our brokenness before God. This advances us toward the goal of knowing Him because a broken spirit dissolves the wall of self-sufficiency that separates us from God. If we're to develop a familiar friendship with God, we cannot separate ourselves from Him during pain or temptation. The lifetime process of transformation involves God purging us of our tendency to push Him away and His wooing us into union with Him and His loving will for the world.

In the New Testament, it was the broken who came to know Jesus. Think of the woman who had hemmoraged for twelve years, desperate, having spent all her money but finding no cure. Coming up behind Jesus, she quietly felt the edge of His cloak (Mark 5:25-34). Like her, we can use our brokenness to finally accept that our bag of tricks for living life is not nifty enough. No amount of self-help books will rescue us. No more

> *If we're to develop a familiar friendship with God, we cannot separate ourselves from Him during pain or temptation. The lifetime process of transformation involves God purging us of our tendency to push Him away and His wooing us into union with Him and His loving will for the world.*

"looking good kid" facades—we freely admit our pain and temptation to God. Our failures strip us of our self-protection, making us vulnerable to God, just as the cured woman fell at Jesus' feet, trembled with fear, and told Him the "whole truth" before the crowd of people (Mark 5:33).

Perhaps you can accept that we can find closeness with God in times of irritation and anguish, but you wonder what they have to do with *enjoying* God's presence. Enjoyment comes from receiving pleasure, but it also comes from appreciating the benefits deepening our intimacy. When we confess our shortcomings to God, we can enjoy His presence because we know that God's love envelops us in spite of our flaws. No one else so completely understands, loves, and challenges us. This familiar friendship doesn't take away the pain or temptation, but it gives us the strength to stand firm.

QUESTIONS TO PONDER, EXPERIMENTS TO CONSIDER

In what circumstances are you most tempted to stop talking to God? If you were to talk to Him in those circumstances, what would you want to hear from Him?

———

When, if ever, have you felt perplexed by God (or by what was happening in the world)? In what ways did you lay that confusion before God? How could you do that in the future?

———

Which, if any, of the lines below give words to anguish you have felt?

I run to you, GOD; I run for dear life.
    Don't let me down!
    Take me seriously this time! . . .
Be kind to me, GOD—
    I'm in deep, deep trouble again.
I've cried my eyes out;
    I feel hollow inside.
My life leaks away, groan by groan;
    my years fade out in sighs.
My troubles have worn me out,
    turned my bones to powder. . . .
Desperate, I throw myself on you:
    you are my God!
Hour by hour I place my days in your hand,
    safe from the hands out to get me.
Warm me, your servant, with a smile;
    save me because you love me. . . .
What a stack of blessing you have piled up
    for those who worship you.
Ready and waiting for all who run to you
    to escape an unkind world.
You hide them safely away
    from the opposition. (from Psalm 31, MSG)

10

Enjoying God Between the Big Moments

C arol was reluctant to talk about prayer. When Margaret, her mentor, asked her if she had times to be quiet or places that seemed safe and close to God, Carol mumbled that she didn't pray enough and she didn't pray right. Margaret attempted to draw Carol out by mentioning that at times her own prayers seemed mechanical and dry, but even then she sensed that God was close and prayer seemed real.

To this admission, Carol replied, "I pray the Connecticut Turnpike. I use the toll booths as markers." Her daily commute was a time of prayer, with each booth reminding her of another topic to pray about, but she felt it didn't count. She thought she should be doing something more spiritual, and that her aging Toyota could not qualify as a holy space.[1]

When God becomes a constant companion, every corner of life is occupied by the sense of God's presence. There's so much to say to God and to listen to God about that it's no longer boring to wait for an appointment. Even filling the gas tank of a car presents possibilities for conversation with God:

- "Thank You for enough affordable energy."
- "Please help developing countries find ways to afford more resources."
- "Watch over the people I share the road with—the distracted business executive, the distraught parent, the excited teenager."

Becoming intentional about enjoying God's presence invites God to invade the in-between moments of life. Any place can be a holy space—even the bathroom. A friend who has suffered a great deal of pain from endometriosis finds the bathroom to be her best place to interact with God. There, doubled over in pain, she can say what she needs to say and find relief.

Unplanned prayers fill our lives. Author and minister Frederick Buechner describes them: "The ah-h-h-h! that sometimes floats up out of you as out of a Fourth of July crowd when the sky-rocket bursts over the water. The stammer of pain at somebody else's pain. The stammer of joy at somebody else's joy. Whatever words or sounds you use for sighing with over your own life. These are all prayers in their way."[2]

LIVING IN THE PRESENT MOMENT

In-between moments are usually considered unimportant transitions during which nothing happens. Our culture is so addicted to productivity that a moment isn't worthwhile unless we're completing a task or discovering a new insight. It's as if the real thing is happening somewhere else, and we must go there to find it.

This isn't so. Developing eyes for things eternal helps us understand that even when nothing is supposedly happening, God is delighting in us and working His redemption in us. One moment is not more important than the next. For example, I now see that the hours and days before a speaking engagement when I pray for listeners are just as important as the moments I'm in front of people speaking. These times of focused prayer change listeners and how they hear. They build my sense of God's purpose, so I speak with greater aspiration and determination.

As we become more conscious of God's companionship, we pay more attention to the present moment. Our problem is not lack of time, but failure to value the moment and to see God at work in it. To relish this present moment instead of dwelling in the past or muddling over the future opens our ears to hear what God might be saying to us.

> *Developing eyes for things eternal helps us understand that even when nothing is supposedly happening, God is delighting in us and working His redemption in us. One moment is not more important than the next.*

Living in the present moment means that I value the processes of life as well as the products. When I plant a magenta bougainvillaea, I'm not only adding color and beauty to the landscape, but I'm also having a good time interacting with God's creation. I relish God's presence as I crumble the earth between my fingers, meet up with rocks and worms, and watch my cuticles become ragged.

The growing friendship with God helps us move through life listening to a steady inner tempo instead of the drumbeat of circumstances. It was said of Brother Lawrence that "He was never hasty nor loitering, but did each thing in its season, with an even, uninterrupted composure and tranquillity of spirit."[3] That way, we can tune into the pearl-of-great-price words in the midst of the costume jewelry of urgent messages.

Get real! someone may think. *Sometimes I'm so blank—how can those in-between moments count for much?* Trying to maintain a constantly high level of feeling or understanding is not important. In moments when the mind is dim and the heart is tepid, we can perform the valuable task of *resting* in God's presence. God showed high priority for rest by not working on the seventh day of creation, and He guaranteed that our hearts can rest in His presence (1 John 3:19). In fact, His presence is a source of rest: "My Presence will go with you, and I will give you *rest*" (Exodus 33:14-15, emphasis added). Over and over,

God uses rest-related images to describe His relationship with us: we are to *abide* in Christ (John 15:4-10, KJV); the church comes together to be God's *dwelling* (Ephesians 2:22); God was Israel's *dwelling place* (Psalm 90:1). Being able to rest in God's presence—lie in the sun, take a nap, daydream at our desk— is one more way of making our home with God (John 14:23).

MORNING AND EVENING RHYTHMS

Abiding in Christ develops a rhythm of its own more easily when propelled by morning and evening patterns. Donald G. Bloesch writes, "Luther suggested that prayer should be 'the first business of the morning and the last at night.' He advised: 'Cultivate the habit of falling asleep with the Lord's Prayer on your lips every evening when you go to bed and again every morning when you get up. And if occasion, place, and time permit, pray before you do anything else.'"[4]

A word of caution about respecting one's body rhythms is appropriate. Plenty of us who are night people wake up slowly, and we have felt undue guilt that we don't think about God when awakening. Instead, we may need to ooze into the day with a simple acknowledgment of God's presence. As the morning unfolds, we can offer to the Lord the day's schedule—the scary risks, the emotional stretches, the boring tasks: "Every morning I lay out the pieces of my life on your altar and watch for fire to descend."[5]

The quiet moments before sleep are an ideal time to ask, Where was God in this day? This is also a time to resonate with gratitude on the day, recalling tasks, welcoming smiles, or delightful stories told. We can thank God for God, and His unending companionship throughout the day.

Instead of feeling guilty if we "fall asleep on God," we can count it as a credit that God can bring rest. Brother Lawrence went so far as to insist, "Those who have the gale of the Holy Spirit go forward, even in sleep."[6] Words from hymns and worship songs may play in our thoughts through the night and continue their rhythm when we awaken.

71

RHYTHMS THROUGHOUT THE DAY

Between morning and evening, tiny Sabbaths occur all day long. Some Christian traditions have structured these Sabbaths into seven times of prayer scattered throughout the day. These are called the Daily Office, and psalms are used as prayers.[7] (The term *office* is derived from the idea that prayer is our work.) Based on the verse "Seven times a day I praise you for your righteous laws" (Psalm 119:164), the Daily Office occurs at such times as daybreak, 6:00 A.M., 9:00 A.M., noon, 3:00 P.M., dusk (or the end of the workday), and before bed. These moments of prayer "punctuate the day, corresponding both to natural rhythms as well as to events in the life of the historical Christ."[8] We may want to follow that tradition or find Sabbaths within the natural rhythms of our day—before rising, parking a car at work, coffee breaks, noontime, dinnertime, moving from one task to another. Every transition is a time for a comment to God ("I don't like meetings anymore!"), a request ("Please help me remember . . ."), or a question ("How can I show love to a friend?").

> *Friendship with God is not only possible, but it is God's will: "I no longer call you servants, because a servant does not know his master's business. Instead, I have called you friends, for everything that I learned from my Father I have made known to you" (John 15:15).*

It's easy to see why psalms are the prayers chosen for the Daily Office. These slim, unsophisticated scriptural prayers teach us down-to-earth patterns for heavenly conversations:

- effervescing with thanks for deliverance from yet another difficult situation;
- honoring and applauding God for His relentless love, quiet power, and mysterious majesty; or
- pouring out the soul in anger and anguish.

These are things that friends do together, are they not? Friendship with God is not only possible, but it is God's will: "I no longer call you servants, because a servant does not know his master's business. Instead, I have called you friends, for everything that I learned from my Father I have made known to you" (John 15:15).

You know you have a real friend when the two of you can pass time quietly doing nothing and saying nothing clever. It's enough to be together. Having a friendship with God means that we can relax with Him and enjoy His company in the in-between moments all day long.

QUESTIONS TO PONDER, EXPERIMENTS TO CONSIDER

What in-between moments are most boring for you?

————

Do you have a rhythm of prayer in place already—a time of relief during the day when you utter informal prayers?

————

Try using these morning prayers from John Baillie's *A Diary of Private Prayer* when you first wake up:

- "Yet let me not, when this morning prayer is said, think my worship ended and spend the day in forgetfulness of Thee. Rather from these moments of quietness let light go forth, and joy, and power, that will remain with me through all the hours of the day."[9]
- "Grant that in every hour of [this day] I may stay close to Thee."[10]

CHAPTER

11

Asking God Questions

On the advice of a wise teacher I asked God, "What do I need to know?" I laid this question before God as I sat on the swing in my backyard, agreeing to be attentive for the next few minutes or hours or days. That night I dreamed about a family member who was angry. I had talked with her a great deal, trying to help her resolve her feelings, but she would have none of it. In my dream, I was fretting over her when she suddenly whizzed by me on ice skates, smiling and waving. Still dreaming, I asked God, "Is she going to be okay? Should I stop worrying?" She whizzed by me again, still waving.

I told my husband about my dream the next morning, and we agreed that I had gone off into the Twilight Zone for sure. We also agreed, however, that I should stop trying so hard to help her. Maybe I was trying to "fix" her when she needed to work it out with God. Could I trust God?

That day was Mother's Day, and our church distributed bookmarks to the women present. The women around me received bookmarks with clever cartoons, but mine had only these words on it: "Let go and let God." After church, I talked with a friend whose husband was dying, and she told me that she could help him most by not trying so hard to help him. Everything around me seemed to broadcast: Let go!

I don't know that these were messages from God, and I don't know that they weren't. I do know that asking God questions opens us up to hearing truth we are likely to miss. We contemplate what God might be telling us today or has been telling us for years. The day before I asked my question I was filled with worry about my relative's anger. After asking my question, I was ready to talk if she needed me, but to trust God to do the rest.

QUESTIONS IMPROVE THE RELATIONSHIP

Posing questions to God is an important part of our relationship with Him. It goes against what we've learned in our culture about being self-sufficient. We're supposed to find the answers ourselves — dig up facts, make evaluations, and produce a bottom-line solution. But as we become companions of God, we realize that human knowledge is finite and limited. We admit we can't find all the answers and that God's input gives light and heat to otherwise mediocre accomplishments. Submission to God is never easy to learn, but when we start asking God questions, we embark on a radically different way of life.

Early in his career, King David of the Old Testament was good at "inquiring of the Lord." Once when the Philistines encamped as if to attack Israel, David inquired after God for a response. The commonsense answer was obvious: attack, or at least be ready to defend Israel. Yet when questioned, God told David not only to attack but also to circle behind the Philistines and attack in front of the balsam trees because "as soon as you hear the sound of marching in the tops of the balsam trees, move quickly, because that will mean the LORD has gone out in front of you to strike the Philistine army" (2 Samuel 5:23-24). How exciting it must have been to participate in something in which God, your companion, goes out in front of you and does the heavy work. Going out of the way to ask God questions focuses and refines the commonsense answer and fills it with God's power and purpose.

So at any given moment, we may launch two or twenty questions into the air — Is this a wise purchase? How can I be a better friend to my aging mother? How should I approach this business associate who intimidates me?

The question, What do I need to know? may be answered several ways. God might make new information clear or simply help you figure out exactly what information you need to search for. Other times, God reminds us of what we already know. Once when I found myself wanting to avoid a certain friend, I asked God, "What do I need to know — that I probably already know?" A few days later when I was teasing my husband about watching too much football on TV, he said, "What about that saying you like — 'I clean up my side of the street and you clean up yours'?" His words stayed with me and reminded me of the wisdom I needed with my friend. Her views on social issues were different from mine and, to be quite honest, I wanted her to change her views! But her opinions were her "side of the street." My side of the street was to speak up when appropriate, but not to change her mind.

Another key question to ask God is, What next? Instead of drifting with no goals or striving for self-imposed goals, we may ask, What shall I turn my attention to next? Which avenue of service should I focus on next? Which of the twenty-six books stacked on my nightstand should I read next?

Frank Laubach wrote, "When we ask Christ, 'What next?' we tune in and give Him a chance to pour His ideas through our enkindled imagination."[1] To promote this practice of seeking, a college in the Midwest offered professors only a one-year contract no matter how long they had been teaching there. They wanted their professors to stay open to God's possibilities, to keep asking God, "What next?" instead of assuming they knew the answer.

As our relationship with God grows more intimate, we feel more free to ask the tough questions. The psalmists asked many questions that began with "How long . . . ?" (twenty-two!) and "Why . . . ?"

- Why is life the way it is? ("Why do the nations conspire and the peoples plot in vain?" [Psalm 2:1])
- Why are You the way You are? ("Why, O LORD, do you stand far off? Why do you hide yourself in times of trouble?" [Psalm 10:1])
- Why are You doing what You are doing? ("Why have you rejected us forever, O God? Why does your anger smolder against the sheep of your pasture?" [Psalm 74:1])

When the answers to these questions elude us, it may be that we need to ask a more foundational question, What is it within me that needs to change? The answers to our original question won't make sense to us because we need to grow in humility, generosity, or self-control. Asking this foundational question then helps us cooperate with God in transforming our character.

RELINQUISHING CONTROL

This sort of questioning does not insist on a deadline for answers. That's because the benefit of asking these questions is not to obtain answers as much as to open dialogue and build a relationship with God. Madeleine L'Engle communicated this truth through a conversation between two fictional characters, a teenager and her mother.

> Suzy still sounded angry. "Prayer didn't keep Jeb from being hit by a motorcycle. It didn't stop Grandfather from having leukemia."
> "Prayer was never meant to be magic," Mother said.
> "Then why bother with it?" Suzy scowled.
> "Because it's an act of love," Mother said.[2]

Within our loving conversation with God, we lay questions on the table, waiting as long as it takes for impressions, convictions, clarity of thought, peaceful understanding, or helpful words from others.

77

All that asking, seeking, and knocking has a way of shaping our desires. For example, when you ask yourself, *Should I enroll in this class?* a number of dynamics are at work. First, it creates a place for your conscience to speak—Is this a wise use of funds? Are more frugal learning opportunities available? It also prods you to examine your passions, which, if you're keeping company with God, are slowly being invaded by the Holy Spirit. Does this class have something to do with the God-given desires of your heart? Are you considering this because you think it has something to do with a job God is leading you to? Are you using the busyness of attending class to create frenzied activity so you won't notice relationships that need repair? All these character-building, life-shaping questions flow out of a simple scheduling question directed to God.

> *As we grow in our trust of God's presence, we become more willing to live our lives in the shape of a huge question mark.*

This back-and-forth wrestling with God eventually results in a heart that trusts God. "We learn to ask God to think His thoughts in us," wrote Frank Laubach. "Instead of telling God what we want from Him, we ask Him what He wants us to do."[3] We try to align ourselves with God's will rather than convincing God that what we want is a good idea.

As a college freshman, I had an older friend who prayed that if her relationship with her boyfriend was not going to help her relationship with God, they would break up. I was appalled—why invite God to mess up a good thing? But I could see that she trusted God in a way that I did not. She knew what it meant to wrestle with God—asking questions, seeking His ways—and so she trusted Him enough to hold the person she loved with an open hand. I had not yet experienced God to that extent, so her into-Thy-hands approach frightened me.

As we grow in our trust of God's presence, we become more willing to live our lives in the shape of a huge question mark.

ACTIVE WAITING

After posing questions, we wait for answers in the time-honored way of those who received God's promises. Abraham and Sarah waited for a son to be born; Joseph waited for his dreams to make sense; Ruth and Naomi waited in poverty for a kinsman-redeemer. Waiting is not so agonizing, so dull, or so grating if we have God as a companion.

Besides, this sort of waiting is not passive. It is alert, active, and receptive, full of energy and commitment. Just as we're reminded to stay awake and alert for the Second Coming, we need to stay awake and alert for God's presence in the events around us. The stage is set and the players are ready. When God raises the curtain, we're not surprised—or not quite as much, anyway. Dallas Willard writes, "God wants to be wanted and to be sufficiently wanted that we are *ready*, predisposed, to find him present with us."[4]

Active waiting gives us ears to hear. If someone had told me not to worry about the angry relative I mentioned earlier in the chapter, I would have said, "Oh yeah, uh-huh, I know that." But by asking God what I needed to know, I prepared my ears to hear the truth that my mind already knew but my heart had been unwilling to follow.

Alertness to possible answers to our questions gives us wisdom to see things we might otherwise miss. Holy coincidences occur. Scripture we skipped over yesterday seems to shout our names today. Information suddenly appears in books we're reading. Strangers make comments that answer questions they don't know we're asking. Events that seem to happen by chance fit into God's plan for the education of our souls. What looks like a catastrophe is actually a burning bush from which God is speaking. Others tell us the battle is doomed, but God's presence trains us to see Him everywhere—just as Elisha was the first to see the heavenly chariots on the hills waiting to win the battle (2 Kings 6:16-17).

The process of asking God questions is similar to when, as a high school student, you considered having a talk with the

79

only teacher who made sense to you. You packed up your books, paused at the teacher's open door, and wondered, *Should I ask this person what I should do? Can I trust this person?* God is the Teacher who is never absent or too busy or too fed up with kids. This Teacher delights in our questions and is sure to give us what we need.

QUESTIONS TO PONDER, EXPERIMENTS TO CONSIDER

What would be a good breath prayer to let yourself and God know that you are alert and actively waiting for answers to your questions?

———

Try asking God, "What do I need to know that I already know?" and see what happens.

———

What are some of the noises of the world that confuse you? Pray with me the words of John Baillie:

> O God within me, give me grace today to recognize the stirrings of Thy Spirit within my soul and to listen most attentively to all that Thou hast to say to me. Let not the noises of the world ever so confuse me that I cannot hear Thee speak.[5]

CHAPTER

12

Dreaming God's Dreams

When Hudson Taylor, missionary to China, returned to his home in England in 1874, he faced the possibility of never again being able to walk. For many months he laid on his back, able only to move from side to side by grasping a rope fixed over his head. Prostrate in his weakness, he could not write letters, but he could dictate them. With a map of China secured to the wall at the foot of his bed, he prayed and planned for developments worthy of God. Under these conditions Taylor launched his appeal for eighteen recruits to enter the nine still unoccupied provinces of China.[1]

If you spend enough time with someone, you begin to sense that person's dreams. In daily conversations with God, we begin to understand God's dreams for us. This process begins by asking those important questions, *What next? What are Your dreams for me? What is it You're doing in this world that I need to align myself with?*

Hudson Taylor understood God's dream for him as he built a fast friendship with God. He adopted several scriptural phrases as his mottoes, and they seemed to function as breath prayers: Ebenezer (Hitherto hath the Lord helped us [1 Samuel

7:12]); Jehovah Jireh (The Lord will provide [Genesis 22:14]); Jehovah Nissi (The Lord my Banner [Exodus 17:15]).[2] Once he knew what God's dream for him was, he plastered it on the wall in front of him. Nothing, even sickness, could keep him from dreaming of evangelizing inland China.

Taylor is also a good example of how loving God and pursuing God's purposes are inseparable. As our love for God grows, His interests become our interests — evangelization of the world, peacemaking in relationships, ministering to the poor and oppressed. This means setting aside one's own agenda and taking up God's agenda instead. For example, a church leader realizes that his goals for church growth are really about himself — building a bigger, better church — so he changes what he does and the focus behind it. Instead of expanding an organization, he looks for ways to equip the church to behave as Christ did on earth: preaching the gospel and helping the hurting.

> *As our love for God grows, His interests become our interests — evangelization of the world, peacemaking in relationships, ministering to the poor and oppressed.*

When we're seeking God's dreams for us, it changes what we do and what we pray. Praying for convenient parking spaces begins to feel self-serving and we wonder how time spent at the shopping mall could be used better to serve Christ's agenda of justice, mercy, and faithfulness (Matthew 23:23). Do I really need a new shirt or should I enjoy some solitude with God, meet a struggling friend for lunch, or mow my neighbor's lawn? More of our days begin with questions like, How do Your purposes for me in this world fit in today's agenda? Am I focusing on the dreams You've put in front of me? The world's dreams for me — buy more, achieve more, be praised more — fade.

GOD'S WILL: TOO PUZZLING?

Seeking God's will has become quite tricky for some in our age. Should I take a job across the country? Should I lead a Bible study at church? It's as if we think God blinks red or green like a traffic signal.

I saw this dilemma clearly when someone who frequently speaks to groups told me that when she receives a request to speak, she prays before giving an answer. I thought that sounded spiritual, but really, did she get a firm yes or no from God? Not exactly, she said, but she explained that she waits and prays because the one time she accepted a speaking engagement without praying, she was later asked to speak on the same date for more money. "See?" she said. "If I had prayed, I would have turned it down and then taken the other engagement." This kind of thinking makes it sound as if prayer is a magic charm that can be used to get what we want. This overlooks the conversations we've had with God about His purposes and dreams and reduces Him to a vending machine — we put in the coin of prayer and receive the prizes our culture says are so valuable: more money, success, prestige. That's for prize seekers; we're God seekers.

Discerning God's purpose for us can be much simpler. God's general purpose is that people come to know Christ. Within that large envelope are the dreams that He has for each of us and the moment-by-moment versions of that dream. We open that envelope every day and tune into the ins and outs of conversations until we have a sense of God reaching back to lead us with one hand while His other hand stretches forth unseen into His will.[3]

How does this hand lead us? Our continual interaction with God changes our character and desires. Asking God questions and thinking His thoughts transform us from people who *do* acts of mercy into people who *are* merciful (Micah 6:8). Showing mercy is not an isolated action, but a part of our character.

As we enjoy God's presence, He prepares us ahead of time to make decisions. In times of solitude we surrender goals, time, career, and service while praying, "Show me what it is You are bringing forth in me." We hold up even those good, supposedly God-led activities to God so He can help us examine our motives.

Then, in seemingly unholy, in-between moments, issues

resurface. God's truths and others' needs beckon and even hound us in the bathtub, in the car, in the hardware store. A part of us keeps tally of the nudges of this still, small voice: "Your child needs . . . ," "Your church needs . . . ," or "Your heart needs. . . ." Then decisions aren't so difficult, but are based on the tally. How does this decision line up with what you've been conversing with God about? What has God been telling you lately? The prayer for direction is easier: *I believe this is what You're saying to me, God. Show me if I'm wrong.* More waiting, more seeking.

EXPLORING GOD'S PURPOSES

Nehemiah was good at investigating God's purposes and pursuing them. After weeping, mourning, and fasting over the broken walls of Jerusalem so much that his boss gave him time off to survey the wreckage, Nehemiah traveled from Babylon to Jerusalem and inspected the walls by night. There, he said, "I had not told anyone what my God had put in my heart to do for Jerusalem" (Nehemiah 2:12). Throughout his adventure in construction management, political maneuvering, and motivational speaking, Nehemiah prayed (Nehemiah 2:4; 4:4,9; 5:19; 6:9,14) and found energy and insight to surmount obstacles.

> *As we experience continual interaction with God—especially expressing our pain and anguish—God makes these "special undertakings" so clear to us that we assume we thought of them ourselves. He allows the things that trouble Him to trouble us.*

Like Nehemiah, we can know God's dreams for us by listening to God speak about His purposes on earth. "The Loving Presence does not burden us equally with all things," wrote Thomas Kelly, "but considerately puts upon each of us just a few central tasks, as emphatic responsibilities. For each of us these *special undertakings* are our share in the joyous burdens of love."[4]

As we experience continual interaction with God—especially expressing our pain and anguish—God makes these "special undertakings" so clear to us that we assume we thought of them ourselves. He allows the things that trouble Him to trouble us. A prayer such as the one prayed by Bob Pierce, founder of World Vision, becomes a litany: "Let my heart be broken with the things that break the heart of God."[5]

What breaks your heart that breaks the heart of God? That pregnant teens feel so helpless? That God's Word is interpreted so poorly so often? That so many peoples are unreached with the gospel? Your answers to that question reveal your "special undertakings." It doesn't matter if they don't seem like a big deal to others if they're the purposes God has put within you. "The inner sense of compassion is one of the clearest indications from the Lord that this is a prayer project for you,"[6] advises Richard Foster. And a prayer project has a way of growing until you can't go another day without participating in it some way.

Hudson Taylor knew his "special undertaking" was to recruit missionaries to penetrate inland China. Some people thought he was foolish at first and tried to discredit him. By the time his work was deemed successful, he was offered other opportunities, but he stuck with his God-given purpose.

In past years, God has made it clear which of His concerns I must focus on because they have broken my heart: helping others deepen their relationship with God, pleading for the poor and oppressed, helping others heal hurts from the past, ministering to pastors' families, and urging the American church to focus on purpose instead of glitz.

When I'm asked to serve or speak or write an article or book, I am still tempted to make my decision based on money and prestige, but I'm learning to say no if it doesn't fit the purposes God has put in front of me. When I was asked to lead women's ministries in my church, I turned it down and led a support group instead. When I was asked to speak about time management, I turned it down and instead accepted an invitation to speak at a retreat focused on drawing people closer to God. Women's ministries and time management are important, but I must concentrate on what I believe God is calling me to do. When we operate this way, God is not a traffic signal flashing green or red lights, but a steady burning flame illuminating the vision He's given us.

Enjoying God's presence doesn't mean having a private party with God while the world wallows in despair. It doesn't mean we never venture off God's lap into the scary path of doing His will in this world. All that lap-sitting focuses us on the Father's business in this world. It gives us the desire and courage to spread understanding and knowledge of God. A secure relationship with God equips us to serve without needing others' praise and to chase something besides what the world thinks is success.

QUESTIONS TO PONDER, EXPERIMENTS TO CONSIDER

Describe a time when you felt led by God—when you had a sense of God's hand reaching back to lead you while God's other hand stretched forth into what He wanted for you.

————

What breaks your heart that you suspect breaks the heart of God?

————

Experiment with this prayer entitled "Think Through Me" by missionary Amy Carmichael:

> Holy Spirit
> think through me
> till your ideas
> are my ideas.[7]

CHAPTER

13

Hearing God

The physical therapist was stunned as she watched her patient do an exercise she had not prescribed. Marie, a stroke victim, had not been able to walk without holding on to the railing in her dining room. But if she walked backward, she could walk without holding on! After a few days with that new skill and confidence, she found she could walk forward too.

Where did she get the idea to try walking backward? the physical therapist quizzed her.

"From God. God told me," admitted Marie, a well-educated world traveler and church planter who herself cringes when someone begins a statement with "God told me. . . ."

God had given Marie other ideas too. The stuttering from the stroke had been so bad that she could hardly stand to hear herself. She was already spending a lot of time in prayer—why not pray out loud? And so she did for two hours every day. What great speech therapy for a public speaker!

Continual conversation with God means that there are moments when God speaks and we listen. Even though it may be scary to think of God speaking to us, it is normal and not weird. Thomas Kelly assures us that "we have all heard this holy Whisper at times."[1]

Sometimes God speaks through a Bible passage that startles you even though you've read it before. You refuse to move on until you've pondered how it speaks to your situation. For example, after her stroke, Marie was reading Psalm 69:32: "The humble shall see their God at work for them. No wonder they will be so glad! All who seek for God shall live in joy" (TLB). It

> Continual conversation with God means that there are moments when God speaks and we listen. Even though it may be scary to think of God speaking to us, it is normal and not weird.

occurred to her that the stroke had changed many things, but it had not changed the great joy she felt in ministry. Before, she had been joyful in her service to God in church work; now she felt great joy in her new ministry of prayer. These small, less than earth-shaking insights feed into a steady stream of transformation so that after interacting with God, we become different people—more conformed to His image.

However, some find that God does not speak to them even in Bible reading. Perhaps that's because they read the Bible to meet an obligation, study for a class, or prove an opinion, but not to meet with God and hear Him speak. A. W. Tozer advised, "[The Bible] is not only a book which was once spoken, but a book which is *now speaking*. . . . If you would follow on to know the Lord, come at once to the open Bible expecting it to speak to you. Do not come with the notion that it is a thing which you can push around at your convenience."[2] Instead of coming to the Bible searching for what we already understand or agree with, it's wise to approach it with the question, What do I need to know?

When pondering God's communication with us, a healthy skepticism is not out of place, however. The messages people claim God has given them often sound too much like their own desires whitewashed in God-talk. Besides, many have claimed God-spoken dates for the Second Coming, but the prophecy has not come true.

Some Christians overreact to these blunders by isolating God's voice to the Scriptures alone. Dallas Willard wrote about this: "Frankly, there is abroad in the world today, and very strongly present in conservative religious circles, a position we may aptly characterize as 'Bible deism.' . . . [It] holds that God gave us the Bible and then went away, leaving us to make what we could of it, with no individualized communication through the Bible or otherwise."[3]

The Bible itself offers examples of God communicating with individuals such as Abraham (Genesis 12), Moses (Exodus 33), Samuel (1 Samuel 3), and countless others, including the entire church group in Antioch (Acts 13:1-4). Here are some other verses to ponder as well.

> I will instruct you and teach you in the way you
>   should go;
>   I will counsel you and watch over you.
>   (Psalm 32:8)

> Listen and hear my voice;
>   pay attention and hear what I say. (Isaiah 28:23)

> Whether you turn to the right or to the left, your ears
> will hear a voice behind you, saying, "This is the way;
> walk in it." (Isaiah 30:21)

> I keep asking that the God of our Lord Jesus Christ,
> the glorious Father, may give you the Spirit of wisdom
> and revelation, so that you may know him better.
> (Ephesians 1:17)

HOW GOD SPEAKS

Some of the most common ways God speaks to us are described by the fictional character Aiden Lucas, a monk, when talking to a minister who was unused to communicating with God.

> "I think we can discount the prospect of a vision complete
> with heavenly choirs and a message written in fire in the

sky," said Lucas. ". . . Watch out for the phrase which keeps recurring on the lips of different people; watch for the incident which strikes the chord of memory, . . . examine every event which occurs in your life and ask yourself if there's something to be learnt even from the most apparently irrelevant occurrence. I'm convinced that even if there's no single revelation, there'll be a succession of signs which will add up to an enlightenment."[4]

Let's look at some of these ways God speaks.

Recurring thoughts. When the same thought presents itself several times, it may be the "candle of the LORD" searching your inward parts and shedding light on your dilemma[5] (Proverbs 20:27, KJV). It's wise to ask God, *Are You saying this to me?*

Not all recurring thoughts act as God's candle, however. We learn to recognize and dismiss the old, destructive tapes— the urge to end our life, to consider life hopeless, to want to get even, to consider ourselves nice little Christians. From the Word of God, we know these are not the words of God.

New ideas. John Powell, priest and professor at Loyola University, writes, "The Lord puts his ideas into my mind, especially his perspectives, he widens my vision, he comes to fill me in that quiet time and he fills me with his power and his presence."[6] Writer Linda Wagner notes that "into the quiet comes a fresh idea on how to approach a problem, a reminder to follow through on some commitment, or a sense of the best way to organize the day or week ahead."[7]

Fictional characters. Character transformation is best learned within relationship, and as we live with characters for a few hundred pages, they can show us who we are or who we could be. We may even sense God speaking through the character's behavior, asking us, Do you see which of this character's faults are your faults? Do you see what I could do with you if you were willing? Do you see what I have already accomplished in you?

Here are some characters through whom God has spoken to me because they illustrated biblical principles in an unforgettable way:

- Meeting Owen Meany (*A Prayer for Owen Meany* by John Irving) convinced me that God gave me a purpose for my life just as Owen had been given a purpose. Owen relentlessly pursued this purpose, and so can I.
- Meeting Irving Stone's version of Vincent van Gogh (in *Lust for Life*) showed me that God used Vincent's desolate soul, and He could use me too. (Biographies can have the same effect as fiction.)
- Meeting Alyosha (*The Brothers Karamazov* by Feodor Dostoevsky), the "holy fool" among the three brothers, convinced me that it was okay to forget about being a clever "up and comer" and instead become a "fool" for God.

None of these characters are role models, but they're fellow bumblers who can make my mistakes for me and let me absorb what they learn. Sometimes, I see myself so clearly in them that I think, *There but for the grace of God go I.*

Works of art. Every now and then a ballet performance or painting tells me about what has been hidden to me: that peace within is possible, that parents can have great joy in their children, that a job well done is marked by the seamlessness and self-forgetfulness of a skillful dance. Standing one day in the Los Angeles County Museum of Art gazing at the Henri Matisse painting *Woman with a Veil*, I stunned myself and the people around me by sobbing. In the picture, the woman's drained, demoralized facial expression pulled out of me a buried hunk of anger toward a group of people. I thought I'd worked through it and accepted their behavior, but through seeing this painting, I sensed God showing me my angry heart and prodding me to do more forgiving and accepting.

Kinesthetic experiences. Physical activity such as sports or exercise workouts have a way of pressing us and showing us our true selves. While river rafting last summer, I noticed that I felt the same fearlessness I'd had as a teenager canoeing rivers in the Midwest. I dug my paddle into the water the same way; my form was aggressive. On the other hand, last year's trip showed me how fearful I had become. I worried that family members would get hurt, that I would fail, that my house would crumble in an earthquake. I understood this insight to come from God and I placed it before Him, asking for help. I'd already memorized Bible verses about fear, but courage eluded me.

Nothing further happened—as far as I could tell—until ten months later when someone commented on how fearless I looked when I punched the air during my aerobic routine. She was right. I thought about how fearless I felt doing aerobic and walking workouts. It was a strange thought that God might use kinesthetic experiences such as river rafting and aerobic exercise to begin chipping away at my habit of fear.

Journaling. Too many of us think that first you figure out what you think and then you write it down. This is not always true. Many times I don't know what I think (or what God is thinking in me) until I write it. Sometimes what I write is garbled and inappropriate, but it straightens itself out as I pick up speed. I reread it and discover that the words were God-directed after all.

If journaling makes you uncomfortable, consider that you don't have to do it on a regular basis, but only when you choose to do it. You don't have to use correct grammar, write neatly, or use a respectable-looking notebook. A journal is a place to talk to God, to pour out hurts, to write down questions for God, to sit and enjoy wasting time with Him.

God talks to us through these methods listed above in a "language that is clearly understood but not audible—an inner hearing with specific content."[8] He doesn't speak to us so we can revel in having a hot line to Him, but to help us in some way: praying for someone more wisely, changing our priorities, intervening in a way previously unclear to us.

POTENTIAL DIFFICULTIES

Putting God on a timetable. Listening to God is part of our continual conversation with Him. It is not limited to a portion of our quiet time set aside for listening. In fact, designating a certain time to listen to God or demanding an answer by a certain time paints us into a corner in which we have to make up the answer ourselves. Listening to God is a round-the-clock adventure just as talking to Him is.

Limiting God's avenues of speech. God is as likely to speak to us through children as through adults, through enemies as well as allies, through strangers as well as friends. When we're unsure if God is behind the words, we can hold them up and wait for further confirmation.

Putting answers in God's mouth. If we want a certain job or relationship or circumstance badly enough, it's easy to believe that it is God telling us to pursue it when He is not. The heart is so deceitful that it's wise to beware of any "answer" that lines up too closely with what you want it to be. On the other hand, some assume that if it sounds good, it can't be God's idea. Doesn't God want us to struggle or earn everything we get? By practicing the presence of God, we learn to recognize His voice and stop confusing it with our own.

Living in isolation. I often run new thoughts by wise friends to hear their reaction. I may even ask, "Do you think I'm putting words in God's mouth?" or "Is there anything in this that sounds self-promoting (or any of my other pet faults)?"

As I composed a prologue for a book I was writing a few years ago, I sensed I should include a conviction I value. It felt right. I wrote it down, got it ready, but wondered if it was appropriate after all. Risking the loss of face, I called someone I respected but didn't know well, and asked his opinion.

"Let me read this to you," I said, "and then tell me if this is God getting His message across, or if this is just 'Jan-stuff'— something that doesn't fit but I'm including just because I'm eager to express my opinion."

I read the paragraph, and this respected person said gently, "I agree with your point of view, but you don't *need* to include this. It's probably 'Jan-stuff.'" I thanked him and deleted it from the prologue. We often think God is using us to reform the world when it's only a matter of our wanting to ventilate our opinions.

93

Seeking the spectacular. Dallas Willard stresses the superiority of the "still, small voice" within the silence of our minds.

> Many who claim to speak for God refer to their visions, dreams, and other unusual phenomena or to their vague impressions or feelings but with no clear, sane meaning. This does not mean that they are not truly spoken to. But Moses was spoken to directly, "mouth to mouth," or *conversationally*. His meaning when he spoke for God was, therefore, always specific, precise, and clear.
>
> When the spectacular is sought, this is because of childishness in the personality. Children love the spectacular and show themselves as children by seeking it, running heedlessly after it. It may be given by God, even may be necessary, because of our denseness or our hardheartedness. However, it is never to be taken as a mark of spiritual superiority. Those who are advanced in the Way of Christ never lightly discuss the spectacular things that come to them or, especially, invoke them to prove that they are right or "with it" in some special way.[9]

Ignoring basic good sense. Keep the following principles in mind when you believe you hear God speaking to you.

- God won't reveal to you anything that is contrary to His nature. It probably isn't God telling you never to speak to your mother again or to take a job only because it pays more.
- Steep yourself in Scripture. This is a primary way God speaks to us, and it serves as a yardstick for all other communication.
- "Don't force yourself to hear," advises author Linda Wagner. "If there is silence, be still and know that He is God whether or not you 'feel' or 'hear' Him. If what you hear becomes the primary reason for being with Him, hearing becomes the focus of your relationship. This is a type of idolatry. For your own good, He may

withdraw until you again long for and seek Him only. On the other hand, remember that there will be natural silences."[10]

- Don't expect to hear dynamic, incredible insights. Be faithful in pouring yourself before God because God is the one you love, not because you want stirring insights.

Is silence an answer? "If we know how to listen, God will normally tell us something when he does not give us our requests," writes Dallas Willard. "The Lord was not silent to Paul, even though he turned down his request: *'And he said unto me,* "My strength is sufficient for you; for my strength is made perfect in weakness"'* ([2 Corinthians 12:9], italics added). God is not impassive toward us, like the pagan idol, but calls us to grow into a life of personal interchange with him that does justice to the idea of our being his children."[11]

But what if I don't hear God? People become discouraged when they believe they're not hearing God. Martha Thatcher writes, "Herein lies the root of our discouragement: We are listening for some*thing*, not some*one*. We are, as it were, trying to hear the *voice* of God, not the voice of *God*. This deviation of focus is subtle but pivotal." When we wonder why God doesn't make Himself more clear or our relationship with Him seems so dry and obscure, that shift is obvious. "These concerns are *issue*-centered, not *God*-centered. They focus on *what* God is saying without a prior focus on *God Himself*."[12] Our task, then, is to seek to know God not because we're hoping for dazzling answers, but because we love Him.

John Woolman, a Quaker reformer, commenting on why he decided to support himself as a simple tailor rather than maintain a prosperous merchandising business, said the real concern of life is "so to pass my time that nothing might hinder me from the most steady attention to the voice of the true Shepherd."[13] This Shepherd's voice is the voice of our Parent telling us what we need to know.

QUESTIONS TO PONDER,
EXPERIMENTS TO CONSIDER

Name some people through whom God has spoken to you.

———

Through which unconventional means (fiction, kinesthetic experiences, and so on) has God spoken to you? Describe them.

———

In what ways do you need to obey, meaning listen, better?

Being Present for Others

I took a deep breath as I entered the ballroom. There I was, trying to shake my shyness as I attended a networking meeting
with two hundred therapists from three counties. As a member of the press, I have to do this sort of thing, but I don't like
meetings that eat up my workday.

I picked up my name badge and reflected on my habit of
praying for each person I talk to. *Could I pray and schmooze at
the same time?* I queried God. *With two hundred people?*

As I tried it, one person at a time, I forgot to consider
whether he or she was a useful contact. I enjoyed hearing about
each therapist's interests. Before lunch, I began calculating how
I could sit next to someone who could further my career, but
dismissed it and picked a spot haphazardly. I ended up next to
a wizened old therapist, and we threw ideas back and forth,
including thoughts about faith. I don't know if I made any crucial press contacts that day, but I do know that I had more sig-
nificant conversations than any of the other meetings I've
attended there.

Enjoying God's presence as we interact with people teaches
us to be present for people and to focus on who they are and

what they're saying. It's also more fun than "working the crowd" and more calming for anyone with a trace of shyness.

WORKING UNDER COVER

Conversing with God this way is, in fact, our primary ministry to people. In *The Contemplative Pastor,* Eugene Peterson describes the subversive Christian whose outward role is a "cover" for the true role of pray-er. Pastors, for example, have been hired to preach sermons and lead stewardship campaigns, but their true role is to pray for the flock. "Instead of practicing prayer, which brings people into the presence of God, [pastors] enter into the practice of messiah: we will do the work of God for God, fix people up, tell them what to do."[1] In the same way, we pacify, counsel, and manage friends and family members when our true work is to pray for them, to help them "concentrate on the real but hidden event of God's presence in their lives."[2]

> *Enjoying God's presence as we interact with people teaches us to be present for people and to focus on who they are and what they're saying.*

I've had fun assuming this subversive role of pray-er while volunteering at a drop-in center for the homeless. My official duties vary from working at the message center (answering the telephone, greeting incoming clients, printing names on paper cups) to working at the shower desk (handing towels, shampoo, and soap to clients). These tasks, however, are my "camouflage" or "cover." My primary task there is to pray for clients, volunteers, and whoever else crosses my path. My conversation with God about them is the steady drumbeat among the chaos of a ringing telephone and bantering chatter. Praying for clients doesn't replace giving them a blanket or tennis shoes without holes in the soles, but prayer runs alongside everything I do. And I notice that it keeps me from burnout. I don't quit in discouragement, and I don't feel tempted to grab clients by the T-shirt and yell at them to get a job.

But isn't it distracting to pray while you're trying to get

work done? How can I write a person's name correctly on a paper cup if I'm praying at the same time? I have found that praying for people as I work with them helps me be *more* attentive instead of less attentive. I focus on their words and unspoken messages. I ponder, *Am I hearing their heart? What is it they're not telling me? Can I be patient until they're able to express it?*

CHANGING THE WAY WE VIEW PEOPLE

Keeping company with God as we interact with others also helps us see people the way Jesus saw them. How unusual that the Savior, while on His way to save the life of an official's daughter, stopped to listen to a woman He healed tell Him "the whole truth" (Mark 5:33). Or how amazing that as a boy rolled on the ground and foamed at the mouth, Jesus paused to ask the boy's father, "How long has he been like this?" (Mark 9:21). Why did Jesus conduct this one-on-one, "parents of possessed children" support group when there was a demon to be cast out? He didn't need the information. In both cases, Jesus not only healed physical bodies, but He was also present to each person. By doing so, He created safe places in which anguished people could talk. Jesus liberated one person at a time, although His mission was to save the world.

Viewing people as Jesus did gives us a hidden agenda of prayer. In this "secret ministry," as Richard Foster calls prayer, we can help people immensely. This was Foster's experience:

> Once, in an ordinary committee meeting, I felt moved to pray for one member who seemed weighted with sorrow, even bitterness. I, of course, participated in the discussion, but all the time inwardly I sought to bathe this person in the light of Christ. The meeting was somewhat difficult due to her rather caustic remarks, especially toward two others in the group. But as we prepared to dismiss, this person suddenly began to weep and finally said to the group, "I wish you would pray for me." After she had shared the source of her hurt and anger, the two

who had been verbally attacked gathered around her and prayed the most tender prayer of healing and release. The room seemed full of power and joy.[3]

WELCOMING THE STRANGER

This habit also teaches us to see familiar situations with a different perspective. Here's an example.

> Practically, this means that we go [to church] with our minds set on noticing those whom we meet. . . . As I see Mr. Hubbard walking slowly from the parking lot, I could easily let my eyes pass over him as if he were simply part of the weekly furnishings. Or, I could ask myself, *How does Mr. Hubbard look today?* What cues is he giving me about what his needs might be? Is his glass empty, and might I have some cool, refreshing drink to pour into it? Perhaps I could ask a question about his daughter, who lives on the other side of the country, or make an inquiry about the health of his wife. Yes, that's it; he wants to talk about her and I am available for that.[4]

Conversing with God while talking with others also creates a setting in which we're more likely to listen for people to express their needs. This is one more way for us to be hospitable, to welcome the stranger when we might otherwise bumble along our self-absorbed path.

TURNING THE CULTURE UPSIDE DOWN

Listening for others' needs is a radically different approach to life compared to our culture's impersonal routines. As cash machines replace bank tellers and e-mail messages filter out the quivering voice or exuberant smile, life becomes more detached and isolated. Add competition and rivalry to this mix and a coworker becomes someone who might get the promotion we want, not someone whose needs God is prompting us to meet.

Most of us only half listen to a conversation, waiting for a reference to what interests us or planning what we'll say. Without realizing it, we're thinking, *What's in it for me? How can this person help my work, my ministry, my church, my favorite causes?* It can be difficult to have a deep, openhearted, unjudging reception of the other person. Even our faith attitudes are affected. Acquaintances become objects to be witnessed to; children become recipients of parental quality time. We forget that each person is a deep mystery to be explored and appreciated, someone with whom we can connect and for whom we can pray.

> *We forget that each person is a deep mystery to be explored and appreciated, someone with whom we can connect and for whom we can pray.*

Being aware of God's presence as we interact with others changes us. The desire to use that person for our advancement fades. It's easier to see each person as the one Christ left the ninety-nine to save. Instead of judging friends, we ask God to clarify the path in front of them. We think less about keeping a house and more about building a home, less about running a business and more about building a place of service.

QUESTIONS TO PONDER, EXPERIMENTS TO CONSIDER

Which of your roles (soccer coach, party planner at work, neighborhood watch member, usher at church) give you interesting vantage points for prayer?

————

Think of situations in which you normally push your self-interest. Consider how you could pray for the people you talk with in these situations.

————

Which committees or groups that you belong to could benefit from your praying throughout the meeting?

————

If you were to do one of the above, with whom could you share your experiences?

15

Removing Stones
in the Path

"I have a lot of ideas and plans and energy," says Marcia Means, a member of the pastoral team at a large church. "I'm a take-charge person, known as the networking queen and trend-setter on the staff. That's not bad, but I have trouble being quiet before God and submitting those plans to Him.

"I've learned that having a lot of programs doesn't always glorify God. We can do things that are good, but not the things God wants us to do. I've decided not to do anything unless it glorifies God. I don't want to miss out on practicing God's presence and developing intimacy with Him. Out of that flows a ministry that glorifies Him.

"So I try to listen for the still, small voice of God even if it seems out of step. I may not look as 'with it' now, but I keep wondering, *Can we be individuals who hear God's voice even when it doesn't line up with what others think?*"

Interacting with God as I have described in this book is not merely a habit to be picked up in a few weeks, but a relationship with God that keeps growing. The more we love God, the more we discover that we have the all-too-human problem of a "divided heart" (see Psalm 86:11, Ezekiel 11:19). This chapter examines those difficulties, and the next two chapters explore the root questions behind them.

If God is to dwell in our hearts with no rival, we have to look deeply at our passions and motives. If we do, we will often find that we seek God *and* something else. Before long, this "something else" takes over. Sometimes this "something else" is good: we seek to be a good person instead of seeking God; we seek Bible knowledge instead of God; we seek love, joy, and peace instead of God. But none of these things can replace a relationship with God.

> *If God is to dwell in our hearts with no rival, we have to look deeply at our passions and motives. If we do, we will often find that we seek God and something else.*

So in the rhythm of our lively interchange with God, we ask, *Show me what interferes with my knowing You.* In time, we recognize the things we substitute for God and the influences that interfere with God's voice like static. Over and over, we confess these things to God. These repeated confessions become part of our regular conversation with God. After a while, we detect the phoniness of the substitutes and static more quickly because we've become accustomed to a genuine relationship with God.

SUBSTITUTES FOR KNOWING GOD

Programs and activities. Because our culture (including the church culture) has taught us how to *do* but not how to *be*, we sometimes fill our God-hungry, empty spaces with activities. It's so much easier to set up chairs for a meeting than to spend time in the corner praying. We can become so busy with church that there's no time for God.

People, especially people we love. Commitments to spouse, children, parents, or friends become so central that we devote our energies to them, forgetting that knowing and loving God is the core of our existence. Out of that love for God flows our love for others.

Sometimes we expect the people we love to meet our deep inner neediness—to make us feel better in our anguish and to guess our secret needs and meet them. But only God can fill this inner neediness. Women, especially, suffer from the some-day-my-prince-will-come syndrome, thinking that the man in their life will satisfy their deepest longings. No romance, no marriage, no child will cover our wounds and reassure us that we are loved. Learning to look to God to meet those needs frees us to enjoy those we love without concern for how they fulfill us.

Service. Doing "God's work" can bring such satisfaction and recognition that the work is enthroned instead of God. If at some point the satisfaction fades, burnout sets in. But if our service flows out of a rich inner life with God, we find increasing discernment and encouragement. The service is about our relationship with God, not about our need to be needed. The satisfaction comes not so much from a job well done, but from being a child of God well loved.

Tools for knowing God. Christians today have become spiritual consumers, indulging in one more conference, one more tape, one more book. Substituting the use of spiritual tools for the pursuit of knowing God is subtle. It happens easily because using a tool is a concrete activity that can be measured. You know for certain if you had devotions today, but it's more complex to know if you connected with God during that time. But that was the purpose of the devotions, wasn't it? Or was it? A Bible teacher and friend once confessed: "Bible teachers find themselves gaining knowledge for the sake of knowledge. We're so easily puffed up. We become proud of what we know, yet we don't know God with the intimacy God has designed us for."

An overemphasis on tools puts heavy moralism on us, if not outright legalism. In one church I attended, the entire congregation was encouraged to read through the Bible in a year. I had read the Bible through several times before, and in my burnout, I preferred to have gritty conversations with God based on the Psalms. Church members discussed the day's reading whenever they met, so I was constantly defending my decision. As the year progressed, many people confessed to me that they felt like second-class Christians because they weren't reading through the Bible. This saddened me because Bible reading is such an important tool in knowing God, but it had become an unwritten law for hundreds of people whom God may or may not have been leading to follow this plan.

Spiritual success. It's wise to have an incurable discontent with our petty selves, but the trick is what we do with it. Some of us launch great self-improvement schemes. This is not wise. True character change is not imposed from without, but it grows from within—from that time spent with God, listening to His voice, following His leading.

Beware of trying to be successful at prayer. In the novel *Absolute Truths*, fictional character Lyle Ashworth wrote in her journal of her prayer group's experiments:

> At the beginning I used to think to myself: do our prayers work? Are we a success? But now I know that these are the wrong questions to ask, they're irrelevant. It's not for us to judge how successful we are—and anyway what does "success" mean in this context? To be successful is to do what God wants—and I know that what God wants for us at these times is to *be*, lining ourselves up with him so that he can use us to batter away at the suffering in the world. If we can only *be*, then he can use us and arrange us in the right patterns so that we're playing an active part in his creative purpose, an active part in his redemptive love.[1]

Prayer is a relationship, not a performance.

Experiences with God. Early in my experiment of practicing God's presence, I was advised to be satisfied even if "nothing" happened. It is good to enjoy God's presence just to be *with* Him, not just to get something from it. We look only for God, not for experiences with God. If you seek spiritual fireworks, you'll begin creating them yourself, which will sacrifice the genuineness of your relationship with God.

105

STATIC THAT INTERFERES WITH GOD'S VOICE

It's difficult to be aware of God's presence when certain influences create static. Sometimes their clamor drowns out all inclinations toward God; other times, we mistake these influences for God's voice. God allows this to happen because, "generally speaking, God will not compete for our attention."[2] God wants us to draw near to Him and learn to listen for His voice.

Cultural distractions. Advertisements and newsletters tell us we've missed something important if we don't see this movie, try that restaurant, read this book, hear that speaker, buy this gadget, make that phone call. Striving to be busy and important crowds out hearing the still, small voice.

The New Testament asks us to set aside the frantic craze for doing more, acquiring more, and persuading more and to simply enjoy God. Keeping busy is a subtle way to run from the communion with God we most desire. If we resist this temptation and instead stay close to the heart with an inner solitude, we will find the treasure of enjoying God.

Pursuit of fulfillment. Our culture teaches that happiness flows out of self-worth, which can be cultivated by achieving more and loving one's self more. Biblical teaching reminds us that we will never be enough or do enough (Romans 3:23). (Our brokenness reminds us too!) Our goal is not to find fulfillment, but to "know Christ and the power of his resurrection" (Philippians 3:10), to realize Jesus Christ in every area of life. Out of that love relationship comes more worth than one could find elsewhere.

Self-sufficiency. Striving to be loved and valued leads to what A. W. Tozer calls the "hyphenated sins of the human spirit": self-righteousness, self-pity, self-confidence, self-sufficiency, self-admiration, self-love. To these, I would add self-aggrandizement—making ourselves greater in power and stature than we really are. Tozer said of people in his day: "Promoting self under the guise of promoting Christ is currently so common as to excite little notice."[3] Tozer's book was published in 1948, but self-promotion will always be common because even though we love God, we also love to be noticed. We begin serving God for

106

various reasons, one of which may be our love for God, but then the love of praise creeps up on us. Soon, we would rather be stars than servants.

Marcia Means told me how she came to realize her own self-sufficiency: "It wasn't until we dealt with our grown son living a gay lifestyle that I saw I didn't have the answers for things. In the beginning, I thought I could fix it. I started a support group, but God reminded me, *What if the situation doesn't change?* I had to remember that God was in charge of fixing the situation, and I still have the need to realize God fully in my own life. This was one of the first times I came up against a crisis that I had no control over. It took me a while to function dependent on the Lord."

Inner neediness. It is human nature to be self-obsessed. If we're honest, we all want to be loved, admired, and appreciated. We worry about how we look and what others think of us because we have a deep need to please others. Some of us numb the pain of not being appreciated and fill this neediness with eating, spending, busyness, drugs, and alcohol. These cravings fill our self-talk and crowd out the conversational flow between God and ourselves.

This inner neediness flows out of wanting to be loved and valued, and expecting to find that fulfillment in people and work. Part of what it means to know Christ is to be in the process of learning that God loves and values us no matter what we do. The task is to make that truth so real that it permeates motives, longings, and actions.

CONFESSING WHO WE ARE

One of the greatest helps in conversing with God is to weave confessions of our inner neediness in and out of our moment-by-moment conversations with God. Here are some examples of confessions I've made:

- I'm pushing myself ahead of others.
- I'm eager to look good in the eyes of this influential person.

107

- I'm afraid this friend is going to abandon me if she becomes too successful.

Offering these honest confessions provides the clarity needed to hear God's answer that we are already loved and valued in a way that is deeper and steadier than any human could. As this becomes real, we are free to say to ourselves:

- I will not compete with this person by trying to win the argument.
- I will not try to impress this influential person.
- I will be glad with my friend for her success.

When we dig these stones out of the path, we are freer to enjoy God's presence. We can hear God better as we allow Him to satisfy the inner hunger for ego gratification. Our relationships are more satisfying because we surrender people to God instead of trying to control them. When we feel the urge to acquire bigger and better things, we drop deeper and listen more carefully to what's going on inside. There we find restlessness and hunger that can be satisfied only by intimacy with God. We choose to enjoy God's presence and become satisfied with this creative, loving, liberating communion with Him.

QUESTIONS TO PONDER,
EXPERIMENTS TO CONSIDER

Which of the substitutes or sources of static mentioned in this chapter have you dealt with to some extent?

Which, if any, of the confessions below, written by John Baillie, strike a chord with you?

I confess, O God— . . .
    that often, by concealing my real motives, I pretend
      to be better than I am:

that often my honesty is only a matter of policy:
that often my affection for my friends is only a
       refined form of caring for myself:
that often my sparing of my enemy is due to
       nothing more than cowardice:
that often I do good deeds only that they may be
       seen of men, and shun evil ones only
because I fear they may be found out.

I bless Thee, O most holy God, for the unfathomable
love whereby Thou hast ordained that spirit with spirit
can meet and that I, a weak and erring mortal, should
have this ready access to the heart of Him who moves
the stars.[4]

16

Addressing Deeper Fears About God

"I think that deep down I don't want to talk to God," Tammy confessed to a small group at a church retreat. "I am afraid to have a close relationship with God. I have asked for help and then sinned again so many times. I feel like I'm a disappointment to God. I can't take that. I hate saying, 'God, it's me again. Same story.' So I don't pray."

> *Enjoying God's company is difficult when we have fears about God. Fear causes us to keep our distance from Him—sometimes by staying busy doing things for Him.*

Enjoying God's company is difficult when we have fears about God. Fear causes us to keep our distance from Him—sometimes by staying busy doing things for Him. If our fears about God are numerous, we may choose to visit Him only on Sundays. Intimacy with God doesn't feel right. After all, God wiped out all those peoples in Old Testament battles—who's next?

If we could turn off the lights, hide in the closet, and say what we really feel, we might wonder, *Here I am reading a book about enjoying God's presence. Am I sure I want to be around God all day long? To be honest, I'm afraid that God isn't good or fair. (Doesn't God have mood swings?)*

This fear affects everything about us—our ability to get along with others, our sense of worth, our capacity to serve, our desire to talk to God. If we're serious about enjoying God's presence, we need to explore the truths that soothe these fears.

TRUTHS ABOUT GOD THAT ELUDE US

God Is Mystery

God's ways are not necessarily within our understanding:

> "For my thoughts are not your thoughts,
>   neither are your ways my ways," declares the LORD.
> "As the heavens are higher than the earth,
>   so are my ways higher than your ways
>   and my thoughts than your thoughts."
>   (Isaiah 55:8-9)

Much of what happens on this side of heaven is hidden to us, and even confusing.

The problem is that we expect to understand God, and we become frustrated when we don't. Our culture has taught us that you can understand something if you study it long enough, and once you understand it, you can control it. None of this works with God. Trying to understand God is a futile goal. Trying to control Him guarantees frustration.

Yet it's difficult to have a relationship with someone you don't understand, so how do you relate to God? God has given us the metaphors of parenting and friendship, and they help. Strong parent-child relationships and authentic friendships can grow in spite of an inability to understand each other all the time. A typical child whines and cries when he doesn't get what he wants from a parent. I have done the same thing with God. When what I wanted desperately didn't come to pass, I have assumed that God didn't care how I felt. It took a while to understand that my relationship with God, like any friendship, requires acceptance of the other person, not complete knowledge and understanding of that person's actions.

111

God Is Good

Scripture emphasizes God's goodness and states that evil comes from the prince of this world, not God (Psalm 73:1-2, 86:5, 118:29; Nahum 1:7; John 12:31). Still, we question God's goodness when He doesn't behave in ways that seem good. When His higher, mysterious ways don't make sense to us, we reject Him as unpredictable and capricious.

> *God, also, is not tame or safe by our standards, but that doesn't mean that He is not good in a way that exceeds our understanding.*

Again, the problem is that we expect to understand God. His goodness may not make sense to us because of our human limitations. Can we accept that?

Various characters in the *The Chronicles of Narnia* demonstrate this ability to accept God's mysterious behavior as good even though it doesn't make perfect sense. Regarding the lion Aslan, who represented Christ, the last king of Narnia in *The Last Battle* said, "Aslan is not a *tame* lion."[1] In *The Lion, the Witch, and the Wardrobe*, Mr. Beaver said, "Who said anything about safe? 'Course [Aslan] isn't safe. But he's good."[2]

God, also, is not tame or safe by our standards, but that doesn't mean that He is not good in a way that exceeds our understanding. His lack of tameness and safety also doesn't keep Him from being eager to carry us on His back through dangerous moments and enjoy us in the in-between moments.

God's Anger Is Not Like Man's Anger

People often view God as a projection of their own personality. If, when you get mad, you want to punch people, you may assume God wants the same. If you sulk and turn anger inward, you may act as if God's anger smolders at you.

What is the truth about God and His anger? It is different from man's anger:

> For I am God, and not man—
>   the Holy One among you.
>   I will not come in wrath. (Hosea 11:9)

God gets angry in response to human moral lapses, but He does not have temper tantrums. Unlike us, He manages to be fair even when He's angry. God delights in showing mercy, not in showing off His power in irrational, thoughtless actions (Micah 7:18). That means we are being unfair when we assume God is out to get us each time we do something wrong.

God Is Merciful

Because so much about God is mysterious, it helps to focus on what we do understand about God's mercy.

- God grieves over our sin just as parents grieve over the sin of their children (Genesis 6:6-7).
- God takes no pleasure in the death of the wicked and wants every person to take responsibility for wrong-doing and turn from it (Ezekiel 33:11, 1 Timothy 2:4).
- God understands that humans have difficulty understanding His justice versus mercy, and He allows them to ask questions about it (Genesis 18:20-33).

Our disobedience angers God, but it also breaks His heart. Hosea 11 provides a peek behind the curtain of God's heart. In this passage, God paced back and forth, pondering the punishment of Israel. In verses 1-4, God talked about His affection for the rebellious child Israel:

When Israel was a child, I loved him,
    and out of Egypt I called my son.
But the more I called Israel,
    the further they went from me.
They sacrificed to the Baals
    and they burned incense to images.
It was I who taught Ephraim to walk,
    taking them by the arms;
but they did not realize
    it was I who healed them.
I led them with cords of human kindness,

113

with ties of love;
I lifted the yoke from their neck
and bent down to feed them.

Then in verses 5-7 God moves into a tough-love stance and plans to discipline Israel.

Will they not return to Egypt
and will not Assyria rule over them
because they refuse to repent?
Swords will flash in their cities,
will destroy the bars of their gates
and put an end to their plans.
My people are determined to turn from me.
Even if they call to the Most High,
he will by no means exalt them.

Yet God struggles with this tough discipline. In the next verse He says,

How can I give you up, Ephraim?
How can I hand you over, Israel?
How can I treat you like Admah?
How can I make you like Zeboiim?
My heart is changed within me;
all my compassion is aroused.

Parents go through a similar anguish in disciplining their children. Seeing God in this anguish tends to arouse our trust that He doles out justice and mercy wisely—even when we don't understand it.

Human Knowledge Is Limited

God appears sometimes to be unfair because humans know only a small piece of the story. Suppose you peeked into a neighbor's window and saw that neighbor spanking a child. You might assume that parent was hotheaded. But the truth is that you didn't see the warnings or the flagrant rebellion, so you judge the parent by the minute or two of behavior you witnessed. Regarding Old Testament battles, it's easy to forget how many warnings God gave and how many prophets God sent to Israel and the surrounding nations. Punishment was not arbitrary (1 Samuel 15:6). We don't know the facts about each nation, nor is it the purpose of the Old Testament to explain this to us. Also, keep in mind that God excels in rescuing people behind the scenes. (One example of this is His intervention in the Abraham/Abimelech/Sarah affair. See Genesis 20, especially verse 6.)

Human Concepts of God Can Be Blurred

In Jesus' parable of the three servants, the third servant mistakenly viewed his master as a "hard" man who swindled money and crops from others (Matthew 25:24). As a result, he unwisely hid his one talent in the earth. In the same way, our views of God as a "hard" guy persuade us to bury treasure that is ours, such as the gift of God's presence.

The most frequent distortion is attributing to God the irrational, undisciplined anger of an adult from our childhood. Such relationships build up negative self-talk, which can be confused with the voice of God: You are ugly, you are worthless, you are inadequate. These distortions are not easily corrected, but it can be done through the complex, but interesting process of . . .

- studying the truth about God's character;
- picturing that truth in our hearts;
- building relationships with those who more closely reflect God's grace; and
- developing a conversational relationship with God that is pliable enough to let us air our grievances to Him.

Some may need to rework their image of God if it has been blurred and smudged from life experiences. If certain names for God or metaphors for God produce fear in you, you may wish to use alternates. For example, if a parent image is not helpful, you may want to consider the creator-

115

artwork relationship we have with God. We are His new creation, the work of His hands (see 2 Corinthians 5:17, Isaiah 29:23).

In this chapter, we've looked at the fear that God is not good or fair, and in the next chapter we'll look at another common fear about God. If, in reading these chapters, you sense that your fears in these areas are great, it would be a good idea to tackle one of the many books on these subjects. Your local Christian bookstore can start you in the right direction. These resources can help us find the peace to dwell with God and enjoy His presence (Ephesians 3:17).

QUESTIONS TO PONDER, EXPERIMENTS TO CONSIDER

If you could ask God any question about His "mysterious ways," what would it be?

———

Read Psalm 139:2-5, printed below.

> You know when I sit and when I rise;
>   you perceive my thoughts from afar.
> You discern my going out and my lying down;
>   you are familiar with all my ways.
> Before a word is on my tongue
>   you know it completely, O LORD.
> You hem me in—behind and before;
> you have laid your hand upon me.

———

Check the box below that summarizes your response to this psalm.

☐ I feel secure knowing this.
☐ I feel uneasy knowing this.
☐ I like these ideas, but I probably don't understand or absorb what they mean. (This is the reaction of the

psalmist, who wrote in verse 6, "Such knowledge is too wonderful for me, / too lofty for me to attain.")

———————

What truths do you understand about God that you need to focus on more?

17

Believing God Loves Me

One evening in my third year of leading a support group for people with eating disorders, I noticed that the same theme seemed to emerge each week. In different ways, group members expressed doubt that God loved them. So the next week, I asked them to talk about this, but they all insisted they had no doubts that God loved them.

So I opened the sharing for general topics, and to my surprise, the doubtful comments returned: "God probably hates to hear from me," "God must be mad at me when I think this," and "I don't know how God can stand me. . . ." That's when I realized that many of us are unaware of our insecurity about God's love. I began to look within to see if I really believed that God loved me and to ponder the reason for the distance between us.

Bound up with the fear discussed in the previous chapter (*I'm afraid that God isn't good or fair*) is another fear, *I'm afraid that God doesn't love me.* We don't own up to this fear because we're not always conscious of it. But when we begin pouring our anguish out to God in genuine, frank ways, we wonder if He's compassionate enough to "put up with us." Or we think that learning to hear God better would be a good idea, but what if He tells us to go to Mongolia? Maybe we don't want to hear Him after all—He might force us to do something we hate. If you find yourself reluctant to enjoy God's presence in certain moments of life, that may be a signal that you have fears about whether God loves you.

Yet it sounds so wrong to say that. How can we doubt God's love when we have said and sung, "Jesus loves me"? Quoting the verse "God is love" (1 John 4:8) doesn't mean we truly believe it on deeper levels. Jokes about thunderbolts and comments about God sending problems to "get our attention" or "make us stronger" tell about what we believe. They explain our distant prayer life. Who would want to practice the presence of a Cosmic Cop? Praying can become a matter of putting on our Sunday best for God. Frenzy fills our lives because if we stop running, we may have to face an empty silence or

> *If you find yourself reluctant to enjoy God's presence in certain moments of life, that may be a signal that you have fears about whether God loves you.*

a nagging voice from God. We're not sure if God is out to get us or if God is out to save us.

We struggle to believe that we are the beloved of God. Former Yale religion professor Henri Nouwen, now living in the L'Arche Community of Daybreak in Toronto, Canada, tells about his struggle:

> Though the experience of being the Beloved has never been completely absent from my life I never claimed it as my core truth. I kept running around looking for someone or something that could convince me that I was indeed the Beloved. I was much more eager to listen to the other, louder voices saying: "Prove that you are worth something; do something relevant, spectacular or powerful, and then you will earn the love you so desire." Meanwhile, the quiet, gentle voice that speaks in the silence and solitude of my heart remained unheard or, at least, unconvincing.[1]

The fear that God doesn't truly love us is so foundational that it merits an entire chapter as we look within and ponder what our behavior tells us about what we believe about God's love.

DO I DESERVE GOD'S LOVE?

We've been told we don't have to qualify for God's attention with our good behavior, but it's difficult to believe. To penetrate that barrier, it helps to look at God's behavior with people of the past. For example, imagine Hagar, who despised her mistress, languishing in the desert. While it's true that Abraham and Sarah were unfair to her, Hagar was not faultless. Could we say she deserved God's presence? No.

But there in the desert, God provided a life-giving spring that Hagar did not deserve. She, a fringe member of the household of the chosen, was seen by God and loved by God in her less-than-shining moment. She spoke words that we need to spend the rest of our lives absorbing: "You are the God who sees me" (Genesis 16:13).

But what if you've sinned too much? Jesus told a story of a boy who sinned morally, religiously (what was a nice Jewish boy doing feeding pigs?), and financially in a way that might never be paid back. Jesus created the dramatic scene of the exuberant father running down the trail to embrace the boy in spite of his sin. How did he know his son was coming? Did the father watch from his roof for years or post servants on the perimeter of his land watching for the boy? We know only that the father sensed his son's change of heart and forgave him before he could ask (Luke 15:11-32). God is even more eager for us to turn our focus toward Him and to eagerly welcome us home. "Always, everywhere God is present, and always He seeks to discover Himself to each one,"[2] wrote A. W. Tozer.

This emphasis on love isn't to say that God doesn't demand obedience. God is as tough as one of my grueling eighth-grade teachers who gave us impossible assignments. The difference is that God comes alongside us to walk us through the assignments, knocking at the door during homework time, sitting next to us and helping us find the answers.

Believing God loves us equips us with a clear-eyed acceptance of who we are. When we strut our self-importance, it becomes clear that we want to be loved and valued. God's love tackles us, telling us that we can quit asking what we must do to be loved and valued because His answer is, Noth-

> *God's love tackles us, telling us that we can quit asking what we must do to be loved and valued because His answer is, Nothing.*

ing. He already loves and values us in a way that is deeper and steadier than any human could. In the moments of writhing in pain as a friend moves away or as we agonize over a project that fails, we finally believe God is the Friend who can fill our empty, jagged places inside.

LIVING IN THE TRUTH OF GOD'S LOVE

We struggle to believe this truth because, although our minds accept it, our hearts need time to process it. It takes effort to digest this truth so thoroughly that it echoes within us and lights up our perspective.

We start by soaking in this truth and experimenting with ways to absorb it: contemplating it, doodling it, creating dance steps to it, putting His words of love to music, praying our love back to God—whatever activity weaves it through the layers of the soul. At times, I've listened to songs about God's love for me over and over, letting it wash over me until I'm immersed in it. I often see myself as the prodigal child walking down the road watching my Father run to embrace me, or I sit in a heap of gratefulness as I understand that, like Hagar, I have done nothing to deserve a life-giving well, but God has provided it for me because He will never abandon me.

Soaking in a word or phrase helps us to live in the truth of it. I enjoy soaking in the word *lavish* in the context of this verse: "How great is the love the Father has lavished on us, that we should be called children of God! And that is what we are!"

(1 John 3:1). The word *lavish* communicates to me that there's more than enough love to meet my needs.

Another powerful transmitter of God's love is the compassionate faces of friends accepting us at our worst. As we develop our own symbols of God's love, we can use them to re-immerse ourselves in the truth and pitch our tents there.

I described one of my ways of processing this truth in my book *Healing Hurts That Sabotage the Soul*, coauthored with Curt Grayson:

> A child development specialist advised me to buy a picture of Jesus holding a child on His lap for my daughter so that she would understand that God loves her. In the picture I bought her, Jesus touches the child so gently and holds His hand behind her head. He rubs His bearded cheek next to her cheek and she looks peaceful. Sometimes when I have failed or I feel lonely, I take this picture down from my daughter's wall, bring it to work with me and set it behind my computer monitor. Throughout the day, I look at it and picture myself as the child. I think about how God loves me the same way and it comforts me.[3]

NEW FREEDOM

Working through our doubts about God's lavish love frees us to enjoy God's presence in more corners of our life. No topic is off-limits: sexuality, sports, leisure. We see that God wants to converse with our real self as much as our church self.

The compartmentalization between sacred and secular may fade. If we live with an awareness of God's involvement in everything, we understand that Jesus was doing sacred work not only when He taught in the synagogue but also when as a carpenter He built a table and chairs for a family. The separation of faith from everyday life evaporates. It's not a matter of "taking Christ to work" or "inviting Christ into your home," but of recognizing God's activity in the dailiness of life.

Believing in the heart and gut that God loves us makes it much easier to enjoy spending time with God. As He becomes the tender Friend and wise Parent we've longed for, we gladly "waste" time with God all day.

QUESTIONS TO PONDER, EXPERIMENTS TO CONSIDER

What, if anything, do you need to say to God that you've never said?

———

When do you feel most loved by God?

———

When has God shown you mercy even though you deserved less?

———

If you could create any kind of picture of God and yourself based on the following verse, what would it be? "How great is the love the Father has lavished on us, that we should be called children of God! And that is what we are!" (1 John 3:1).

18

Revamping the "Quiet Time"

John Duckworth, in his book *Just for a Moment, I Saw the Light*, puts a new spin on the traditional concept of "quiet time."

I'd just returned from a convention of Christian bookstore dealers, where my job as an editor was to walk up and down the booth-lined aisles, past endless rows of books and bumper stickers, tapes and key chains, plaques and Scripture sponges. The more I'd seen, the more I'd been bothered by the gimmicks and the hype. I'd used both in my work too. If some of these exhibitors were moneychangers in the temple, so was I.

I left the convention wanting to apologize to God. Not until I got home, sitting in an empty house in the middle of the afternoon, did I feel I could do it properly. I sat on the couch and bowed my head. But for some reason I couldn't pray. My position was wrong, I thought. I'd been thinking of myself more highly than I should, and now I needed to be lower. I kneeled, I couldn't recall the last time I'd done that, but I tried it now. It didn't feel right either. I needed to be lower still.

The only other posture I could think of was bowing down like Muslims did when they faced Mecca. *Too strange*, I thought. I never prayed that way. I couldn't.

Yet a moment later I found myself on the floor, down on my face, my forehead to the carpet. Finally it felt right. I started to pray silently, but stopped. It didn't seem to be a time to talk, but to listen. I waited for a long time, and a verse I'd known for years whispered in my memory: Be still and know that I am God (Ps. 46:10).

It was so simple, that verse. If only knowing God could be that uncomplicated. If only it weren't a matter of devotions, of a stern system of readings and prayers, a long march of ancient laws and sleepy inner monologues to slog through, rain or shine.

Bowed down to the floor that afternoon, I suddenly wanted to know the God who would invite me to do such a thing. I longed to meet the One who could be satisfied with silence, the One whose yoke was easier than reading Leviticus at 4 a.m. I just wanted to be still and know God.

I wanted it so much that the next morning I got up half an hour early and bowed down on the floor again. And the next morning, and the next. I didn't even bring a Bible with me at first. I just cleared my mind and thought about that verse. Soon I found myself wanting to worship this God who was so high above me. I would talk to him a little or think about a hymn. But mostly I was still. Then I brought a Bible and read about this God who told the psalmist and Job and Peter and so many others to be quiet, after which I would be quiet too.

A month of mornings became two, then three. Six months passed, and a year. But it was no achievement. It was eating because I was hungry. It was forgetting the rules and making it up as I went along. It was one of the easiest things I'd ever done.

My morning schedule has changed since then. I've shifted hours and postures, and yes, I've gone for long periods without those times of quiet and worship and reflection. But the gaps don't make me give up anymore. They make me tired. And hungry. But now I know a great place to rest and have a bite to eat.[1]

Some may wonder if practicing the presence of God replaces a set-apart quiet time of devotion. Not necessarily. More than ever, you may long for a great place to rest and have a bite to eat. A little prayer sprinkled here and there isn't enough anymore.

Besides, a quiet time trains us to focus and to hear God — skills necessary to enjoy God's presence. The quiet time is to the Christian as batting practice is to baseball players who practice until their skills are so refined that they automatically swing well in a game.[2] We, in turn, practice our talking and listening skills in our quiet time so that they come naturally to us in the dailiness of life.

> *A quiet time trains us to focus and to hear God — skills necessary to enjoy God's presence. The quiet time is to the Christian as batting practice is to baseball players who practice until their skills are so refined that they automatically swing well in a game.*

Practicing God's presence and enjoying it may mean, however, that our quiet times loosen up a bit — perhaps forgetting the rules and making it up as we go along. We may find ourselves moving out of the closet on occasion and into the park. Many fine books have been written about having timeouts with God, but here are a few often-overlooked activities that prepare us for a daily awareness of God.

LEARNING TO ENJOY SOLITUDE

Solitude is much bigger and better than being alone in the car for a few minutes. Jesus, it seems, couldn't get enough of it. The Gospels are full of Jesus taking personal getaways. His most frequently cited getaway occurred at daybreak when He went out to a solitary place (Luke 4:42) after a day of recruiting follow-ers, driving out demons, and healing people (Mark 1:21-35). When this passage is taught, it is often emphasized that after such a busy day most of us would have slept in, but Jesus was so disciplined that He didn't. The point is well taken, but it also promotes feelings expressed above by Duckworth about the quiet time as something to "slog through, rain or shine."

The text doesn't say what was in Jesus' mind, so consider this alternative. After a day of chaotic, people-oriented service, He would be tired, but because He loved spending time with God the Father, He might also be eager to wake up early the next day and go off to be with Him. After a day of busy ser-vice, I often long for an extended time to be with Him alone. I find I have a lot to say to God and a lot I need to hear. In Jesus' case, the pull was so strong that He didn't worry about the previous day's needy people requiring intense follow-up. Jesus entrusted these new followers and formerly possessed people to God. He seems to have been a Messiah without a messiah complex.

In solitude, our character defects come to the surface. Soli-tude can make us painfully aware of our tendency to grasp at things and strut our egos across the stage of life. Solitude trains us to quiet our cravings and still our distractions, so that in all of life we can be more attentive to God and listen for God to speak.

Solitude changes our character too. Henri Nouwen writes that solitude "molds self-righteous people into gentle, caring, forgiving persons who are so deeply convinced of their own great sinfulness and so fully aware of God's even greater mercy that their life itself becomes a ministry."[3] Spending time in soli-tude helps me handle critics much better. When my husband began pastoring a new church, one woman noted that I had been away teaching at retreats for several weeks in a row and commented, "Her career is more important than the church." Years ago, that would have devastated me. But I have, for years now, lain facedown on my living room carpet asking God if He wants me to speak publicly, and if so, what my focus should be. The answer over the years has been clear: retreats are my

127

specialty. Still, after hearing this woman's comment, I brought it to God for a while. I didn't sense a change in direction, but a change in me. I gained a compassion for my critic that I needed, and I was able to respond with a gentleness that surprised me.

Solitude provides a groundedness in God that keeps us from being victims of other people's opinions. Silence before God helps us see that God can do great things without my fixing and rescuing everyone in need. Any time we sense an anxious emptiness inside, this becomes a signal to spend time with God and listen for His still, small voice. Gradually we learn to do this anywhere under any circumstances.

My greatest help in settling into solitude is a "palms down, palms up" exercise, such as Richard Foster described:

> Begin by placing your palms down as a symbolic indication of your desire to turn over any concerns you may have to God. Inwardly you may pray, "Lord, I give to you my anger toward John. I release my fear of my dentist appointment this morning. I surrender my anxiety over not having enough money to pay the bills this month. I release my frustration over trying to find a baby-sitter for tonight." Whatever it is that weighs on your mind or is a concern to you, just say, "palms down." Release it. After several moments of surrender, turn your palms up as a symbol of your desire to receive from the Lord. Perhaps you will pray silently: "Lord, I would like to receive your divine love for John, your peace about the dentist appointment, your patience, your joy." . . . Having centered down, spend the remaining moments in complete silence. Do not ask for anything. Allow the Lord to commune with you, to love you. If impressions or directions come, fine; if not, fine.[4]

ENJOYING GOD IN WORSHIP

Brother Lawrence worshiped as often as he could,[5] but praise isn't easy for everyone. Trying to teach my kids to praise God when they were small was my best training. My son (as a tod-dler) and I could be heard saying, "Yea, God," to any sunset. Here are some things to experiment with during your quiet time to hone this skill.

Paraphrasing psalms personalizes them for us. "The LORD is my shepherd, I shall not be in want" (Psalm 23:1) becomes "God always watches out for me, nothing scares me" or "The Lord is my security guard" or "my mentor."

Concentrating on God's qualities. It may help to make pictures out of them. For example, God's power becomes more real when we imagine God carefully monitoring each earthquake fault. God's thriftiness makes sense when we observe the cycles of nature — even rotted vegetation decomposes and fertilizes the soil. God's all-encompassing knowledge shows itself as we watch people's needs being met before they know they even have them.

Singing songs to God. Instead of just singing *about* God, we acknowledge God's presence with us by speaking directly to God. When I was nursing my children as infants at night, I kept falling asleep in the rocking chair. Finally I memorized all the verses to the hymn *Great Is Thy Faithfulness*, and before long I was not only awake but belting out words to God, who became my familiar companion in the dark.

Meditating on "majestic" Scripture tunes us into the heavenly realities beyond our earthly experiences. "Sing to God, . . . who rides the ancient skies above, who thunders with mighty voice" paints a powerful picture of our King and Creator (Psalm 68:32-33). Jack R. Taylor writes, "The perspective of praise is none other than the throne room of the universe where we see God sitting on a throne! God reigns! . . . When we see God as he is, we will praise God as we ought!"[6]

SAVORING GOD'S WORDS

"Meditation is simply the art of thinking steadily and methodically about spiritual things," wrote Evelyn Underhill,[7] but we make it more complicated than that. Brother Lawrence's account of how he envisioned himself before God reminds me of the scene in Psalm 23:5 in which we're seated at a table with our enemies:

> I consider myself as the most wretched of men, full of sores and corruption, and who has committed all sorts of crimes against his king. Touched with a sensible regret, I confess to Him all my wickedness, I ask His forgiveness. . . . The King, full of mercy and goodness, very far from chastising me, embraces me with love, makes me eat at His table, serves me with His own hands, gives me the key of His treasures; He converses and delights Himself with me incessantly, in a thousand ways, and treats me in all respects as His favorite.[8]

Picturing Scripture this way stays with us and often rescues us in the dailiness of life. For example, one day I was supposed to be reading, but I couldn't. My husband had just been laid off after we had bought a home with a large California-size house payment. Could my income and whatever income he could generate make these payments? I had written enough about the problem of homelessness to know that many middle-class families ended up on the street. Would that happen to us?

At that moment, a picture appeared in my mind that terrified me. I was flailing away in deep ocean water trying to hoist myself onto a piece of wood from a ship that had just sunk. My face was scorched, my mouth was parched, and my lips were pickled. Were there sharks in these waters?

Some might call this vivid picture an attack of the Enemy, and I suppose it was. But another scene took over the picture in my mind. It was based on years of meditating on Psalm 18:4-19 with its dramatic, Cecil B. De Mille–like rescue scene. I saw verse 5 take shape in my mind:

> The cords of the grave coiled around me;
> the snares of death confronted me.

But God came to my rescue, like John Wayne in a Western or Luke Skywalker in *Star Wars*. In my fearful imagination, the familiar words took shape: I saw God part the heavens, mount the cherubim, and fly. Darkness was His covering. He came with hailstones and bolts of lightning. He shot arrows at the approaching sharks (Psalm 18:9-14).

As God came closer and breathed hard, the sea water parted and I could see the bare ocean floor. Then God reached down from that perch and drew me out of deep waters (Psalm 18:15-16). Finally the familiar memorized verse throbbed inside me:

> He brought me out into a spacious place;
>   he rescued me because he delighted in me.
>   (Psalm 18:19)

I opened my eyes and knew there would be tough financial times ahead, but that miraculous rescues would occur left and right. And in subsequent months, they did. The dailiness of life in those insecure months took on a rhythm of greater faith because of a picture forged in the solitude of my quiet time.

QUESTIONS TO PONDER, EXPERIMENTS TO CONSIDER

If you changed your quiet time in some way, what change would you make?

_____

If God were to change your quiet time in some way, what would that be?

_____

Consider asking God what you need to know about your quiet time regarding:

- enjoying being alone with God;
- praising God using words you use in everyday life;
- being ruthlessly honest with God;
- taking the Scripture you already know and savoring it in meditation.

131

What to Expect on Your Journey

"I must tell you," confides Brother Lawrence, "that for the first ten years I suffered much. The apprehension that I was not as devoted to God as I wished to be, my past sins always present to my mind, and the great unmerited favors which God did me, were the matter and source of my sufferings. During this time, I fell often, and rose again presently."[1]

Before we leave each other, I need to say explicitly what I have implied: by all means, pursue God through enjoying His presence, but *do not strain over it*. Brother Lawrence's above admission of falling so often makes it easier to be gentle with ourselves when we venture through one day, three days, five days without turning our focus back to God. With his example in mind, we can begin again.

Trying too hard to practice God's presence produces discord[2] because striving for this or any spiritual discipline is a mistake. We don't pursue a spiritual discipline—we pursue God. The discipline is never more important than the desire to know Him. If you must monitor the discipline, watch for progress, not perfection.

LETTING GO OF THE NEED TO PERFORM

We cannot accomplish the habit of enjoying God's presence; God accomplishes it in us. "We easily forget that [praying] is a supernatural act which is therefore beyond our own strength and can only be performed by the inspiration and help of grace," wrote Jean Nicholas Grou. "We must earnestly ask God to produce it in us, and then we must perform it tranquilly under his guidance."[3] Instead of fussing, striving, and monitoring, we surrender ourselves to God over and over again. For those of us who are hooked on productivity, this approach is radical.

You know you're straining when you're overly discouraged by your failures. It was said of Brother Lawrence that "he was very sensible of his faults, but not discouraged by them";[4] it could be said of some of us that we are so sensitive to our faults that we are devastated by them.

If you find that you are straining, set aside this practice for a while. Richard Foster suggests asking God for a timeout. "He is gracious as always and understands our frailty."[5] During the timeout, lay this question before God: Why am I trying so hard? Be open to the idea that "the quest for self-perfection is often sanctified introversion. The ideal is to forget self as Mary did, sitting at the feet of Jesus and to gaze enraptured 'full in His glorious face,' listening for His whisper and doing all He asks."[6]

Letting go of the need to perform for God sets our hearts on things above and turns our backs on self-importance. Instead of trying to have an accomplishment-driven relationship with God, enjoying God's presence points us toward:

- resting instead of productivity,
- being silent instead of talking,
- listening instead of giving advice,
- empowering others instead of preaching to them,
- asking questions instead of knowing answers,
- surrendering instead of gritting your teeth,
- giving instead of consuming,

- striving for brokenness instead of upward mobility, and
- gearing down to simplicity instead of gearing up to empire building.

PRAY AS YOU CAN

When you can't pray, ask God to show you what to do. Four days after the Northridge earthquake in 1994, I received a call from an editor-friend asking me if I would write an article about trusting God through the earthquake. That's when I realized I could not recall praying or thinking of God since the quake. I felt guilty. How could it not occur to a Christian, especially one who has been practicing God's presence for years, to pray in a crisis? Sure, I'd been busy cleaning up, hauling drinking water, and running for cover in the aftershocks, but in between I'd stared into space dumbfounded.

After my conversation with my editor-friend, I began offering breath prayers based on Psalm 46:10. At times, I was capable of praying no more than the first two words, "Be still," but the uttering of those words kicked in a hunger for God that made me long to wrap myself in His presence every minute. It was as if I had discovered my lost coin and I reveled in finding it again.

Certain things happen in life that envelop you for days, weeks, and months. These surprises, both good and bad, take over your existence and seem to interrupt your intimacy with God: a parent becomes ill; a child is suspended from school; you fall in love; you get your dream job. But if your relationship with God has become a steady burning flame that is fueled not by information or inspiration but by the person of God Himself, you can ease back into the habit just as easily as you remember how to ride a bike. Treat yourself gently. Begin again with reminders and breath prayers. God's companionship can then save you from despair or keep you sane during ecstasy. In these moments, "pray as you can and not as you can't."[7]

FRUIT WHEN YOU LEAST EXPECT IT

Another thing that often occurs while enjoying God's presence is that God will nudge you into obedience. When you want to exaggerate, to bad-mouth someone, to skip necessary tasks, your intimacy with Him nudges you into doing what's right. God's presence in the moment replaces whatever you were seeking in your self-indulgent behavior. Praying for enemies as you talk with them makes it easier to see them as God's children and have compassion for them. The world is centered less in self and more in God's agenda.

Frank Laubach warned that even though practicing God's presence takes a while to learn, it becomes easier as we go. "After months and years of practicing the presence of God, one feels that God is closer; His push from behind seems to be stronger and steadier, and the pull from in front seems to grow stronger."[8] At times, the wandering heart snaps back into place and the oneness with God returns instantly. Ideas come "welling up from the unconscious, as from a hidden fountain. God is so close then that He not only lives all around us, but all *through* us."[9] We look forward to life in the hereafter with God, and in the meantime, we taste and see that the Lord is good.

My insights are still evolving on what it means to enjoy God's presence. As you walk your journey with God, I'd love to hear from you. Write and tell me what you're learning.

Jan Johnson
c/o NavPress Editorial
P.O. Box 35001
Colorado Springs, CO 80935

Notes

Chapter One: Trying Too Hard

1. Elaine M. Prevallet, S.L., "Dancing Around the Kingdom: Notes from an Occasional Journal," *Weavings* 10, no. 1 (January-February 1995), p. 32.
2. Oswald Chambers, *My Utmost for His Highest* (Westwood, N.J.: Barbour and Company, 1963), p. 40.
3. Thomas à Kempis, *The Imitation of Christ: Selections* (Wheaton, Ill.: Tyndale, 1968), p. 52.
4. Brother Lawrence, *Great Devotional Classics: The Practice of the Presence of God*, ed. Douglas Steere (Nashville: Upper Room, 1961), p. 9.
5. Facts from this paragraph come from the following except when otherwise noted: Brother Lawrence, *The Practice of the Presence of God* (Old Tappan, N.J.: Revell, 1958), pp. 8-9.
6. Brother Lawrence, Revell edition, p. 8.
7. Roberta Bondi, "The Paradox of Prayer," *Weavings* 4, no. 2 (March-April 1989), p. 7.
8. Brother Lawrence, Revell edition, p. 18.
9. Frank Laubach, *Man of Prayer*, The Heritage Collection (Syracuse, N.Y.: Laubach Literacy International, 1990), p. 26.

Chapter Two: Practicing the Presence of God

1. Martin Luther, *Great Devotional Classics: Table-Talk*, ed. William R. Cannon (Nashville: Upper Room, 1950), p. 29.
2. Brother Lawrence, *The Practice of the Presence of God* (Old Tappan, N.J.: Revell, 1958), p. 18.
3. Richard Foster, *Celebration of Discipline* (San Francisco: Harper and Row, 1988), p. 34.

4. Jean Nicholas Grou, *Manual for Interior Souls*, p. 264, as quoted by Douglas Steere in Brother Lawrence, *Great Devotional Classics: The Practice of the Presence of God*, ed. Douglas Steere (Nashville: Upper Room, 1961), p. 8.
5. Brother Lawrence, Upper Room edition, p. 7.
6. A paraphrase of ideas by John Piper, *Desiring God* (Portland, Ore.: Multnomah, 1986), p. 41.
7. Oswald Chambers, *My Utmost for His Highest: An Updated Edition in Today's Language*, ed. James Reimann (Oswald Chambers Publications, 1992), September 16 entry.
8. Jean Nicholas Grou, *Renovare Devotional Readings*, ed. James B. Smith, vol. 1, no. 5 (Wichita, Kan.: Renovare, 1990), p. 2, emphasis added.
9. Saint Augustine, as quoted in Grou, *Renovare Devotional Readings*, p. 2.
10. Theophan the Recluse, *The Art of Prayer: An Orthodox Anthology*, ed. Timothy Ware (London: Faber & Faber, 1966), p. 110, as quoted in Henri Nouwen, *The Way of the Heart* (San Francisco: HarperSanFrancisco, 1991), p. 76.
11. Frank Laubach, *Man of Prayer*, The Heritage Collection (Syracuse, N.Y.: Laubach Literacy International, 1990), p. 234.

Chapter Three: Thinking About You Becomes Praying for You
1. Thomas Kelly, *A Testament of Devotion* (New York: Walker and Company, 1987), p. 59.
2. Elizabeth Goudge, *The Scent of Water* (New York: Coward, McCann Publishers, 1963), pp. 115, 119.
3. James Houston, *The Transforming Friendship* (Oxford, England: Lion Publishing, 1990), p. 234. American edition available from NavPress, 1996.
4. Martin Luther, *Great Devotional Classics: Table-Talk*, ed. William R. Cannon (Nashville: Upper Room, 1950), p. 33.

Chapter Four: Talking to You Means Praying for You
1. Frank Laubach, *Man of Prayer*, The Heritage Collection (Syracuse, N.Y.: Laubach Literacy International, 1990), p. 45.
2. Laubach, p. 240.
3. Oswald Chambers, *My Utmost for His Highest: An Updated Edition in Today's Language*, ed. James Reimann (Grand Rapids: Discovery House, 1992), October 17 reading.
4. Richard Foster, *Freedom of Simplicity* (San Francisco: Harper and Row, 1981), p. 84, emphasis added.
5. *Eerdman's Book of Famous Prayers*, ed. Veronica Zundel (Grand Rapids: Eerdmans, 1983), p. 99.

Chapter Five: Weaving Prayer with Activity
1. Thomas Kelly, *A Testament of Devotion* (New York: Walker and Company, 1987), p. 54.
2. Brother Lawrence, *Great Devotional Classics: The Practice of the Presence of God*, ed. Douglas Steere (Nashville: Upper Room, 1961), pp. 27-28.

3. Javonda Barnes, *A Call to Prayer*, ed. David Butts (Cincinnati: Standard, 1994), p. 84.
4. Tilden Edwards, *Living in the Presence: Disciplines of the Spiritual Heart* (San Francisco: Harper and Row, 1987), p. 24.
5. The suggestions can be found in Ernest Boyer, Jr., *Finding God at Home* (San Francisco: Harper and Row, 1984), pp. 97-98.
6. Brother Lawrence, *The Practice of the Presence of God*, trans. Robert J. Edmonson (Orleans, Mass.: Paraclete Press, 1985), p. 120.
7. Frank Laubach, *Man of Prayer*, The Heritage Collection (Syracuse, N.Y.: Laubach Literacy International, 1990), p. 239.

Chapter Six: Praying Without Words
1. Elaine M. Prevallet, S.L., "Through an Autumn Lens," *Weavings* (May-June 1991), vol. 5, no. 3, p. 23.
2. Brother Lawrence, *The Practice of the Presence of God* (Old Tappan, N.J.: Revell, 1958), p. 35.
3. Jean Vanier, *Community and Growth* (New York: Paulist, 1979), p. 194, as quoted in *Weavings* 8, no. 1 (January-February 1993), p. 5.
4. Dallas Willard, *The Spirit of the Disciplines* (San Francisco: Harper and Row, 1988), pp. 30, 75.
5. Willard, p. 86.

Chapter Seven: Focusing on What's in Front of You
1. Frank Laubach, *Letters of a Modern Mystic* (New Readers Press), as quoted in *Renovare Devotional Readings*, ed. James B. Smith, vol. 1, no. 9 (Wichita, Kan.: Renovare, 1990), p. 1.
2. John Baillie, *A Diary of Private Prayer* (New York: Collier, 1977), p. 61.
3. Baillie, p. 33.
4. Annie Dillard, *Pilgrim at Tinker Creek* (New York: Harper's Magazine Press, 1974), p. 54.
5. Dillard, p. 30.
6. Frank C. Laubach, *Channels of Spiritual Power* (Westwood, N.J.: Revell, 1954), p. 96.
7. *Eerdman's Book of Famous Prayers*, ed. Veronica Zundel (Grand Rapids: Eerdmans, 1983), p. 106.

Chapter Eight: Finding God in Irritating Moments
1. Roberta Bondi, "Friendship with God," *Weavings* 7, no. 3 (May-June 1992), p. 9.

Chapter Nine: Loving God in Anguished Moments
1. Susan Howatch, *Glittering Images* (New York: Fawcett Columbine, 1987), pp. 145-146.

Chapter Ten: Enjoying God Between the Big Moments

1. Margaret Guenther, *Holy Listening* (Cambridge, Mass.: Cowley Publications, 1992), p. 20.
2. Frederick Buechner, *Listening to Your Life* (San Francisco: Harper-SanFrancisco, 1992), pp. 211-212.
3. Brother Lawrence, *The Practice of the Presence of God*, Revell edition, pp. 28-29.
4. Donald G. Bloesch, *The Struggle of Prayer*, as quoted in *A Guide to Prayer*, ed. Rueben P. Job and Norman Shawchuck (Nashville: Upper Room, 1983), p. 108.
5. Eugene Peterson, *The Message: Psalms* (Colorado Springs, Colo.: NavPress, 1994), p. 10.
6. Brother Lawrence, *Great Devotional Classics: The Practice of the Presence of God*, ed. Douglas Steere (Nashville: Upper Room, 1961), p. 31.
7. Elizabeth J. Canham, "Sing a New Song," *Weavings* 4, no. 4 (July-August 1989), p. 20.
8. Norvene Vest, "The Remembrance of God," *Weavings* 10, no. 3 (May-June 1995), p. 39.
9. John Baillie, *A Diary of Private Prayer* (New York: Collier, 1977), p. 9.
10. Baillie, p. 21.

Chapter Eleven: Asking God Questions

1. Frank Laubach, *Man of Prayer*, The Heritage Collection (Syracuse, N.Y.: Laubach Literacy International, 1990), p. 245.
2. Madeleine L'Engle, *A Ring of Endless Light* (New York: Farrar, Straus and Giroux, 1980), p. 289.
3. Frank C. Laubach, *Channels of Spiritual Power* (Westwood, N.J.: Revell, 1954), p. 97.
4. Dallas Willard, *In Search of Guidance: Developing a Conversational Relationship with God* (San Francisco: HarperSanFrancisco, 1993), p. 235.
5. John Baillie, *A Diary of Private Prayer* (New York: Collier, 1977), p. 73.

Chapter Twelve: Dreaming God's Dreams

1. Marshall Broomhall, *Hudson Taylor: The Man Who Believed God* (Edinburgh: R. and R. Clark, 1929), p. 166.
2. Broomhall, pp. 84-85, 123.
3. Frank Laubach, *Man of Prayer*, The Heritage Collection (Syracuse, N.Y.: Laubach Literacy International, 1990), p. 22.
4. Thomas Kelly, *A Testament of Devotion* (New York: Walker and Company, 1987), pp. 149-150, emphasis added.
5. Franklin Graham with Jeanette Lockerbie, *Bob Pierce: This One Thing I Do* (Waco, Tex.: Word, 1983), p. 77.
6. Richard Foster, *Celebration of Discipline* (San Francisco: Harper and Row, 1988), p. 40.
7. Amy Carmichael, "Think Through Me," *Eerdman's Book of Famous Prayers*, ed. Veronica Zundel (Grand Rapids: Eerdmans, 1983), p. 69.

Chapter Thirteen: Hearing God
1. Thomas Kelly, *A Testament of Devotion* (New York: Walker and Company, 1987), p. 159.
2. A. W. Tozer, *The Pursuit of God* (Camp Hill, Pa.: Christian Publications, 1982), pp. 81-82.
3. Dallas Willard, *In Search of Guidance: Developing a Conversational Relationship with God* (San Francisco: HarperSanFrancisco, 1993), pp. 110-111.
4. Susan Howatch, *Ultimate Prizes* (New York: Knopf, 1989), p. 237.
5. Willard, p. 104.
6. John Powell, *He Touched Me* (Niles, Ill.: Argus Communications, 1974), p. 74.
7. Linda Wagner, "Learning to Listen to God," *Discipleship Journal* 73 (1992), p. 52.
8. Wagner, p. 52.
9. Willard, pp. 113-115.
10. Wagner, p. 53.
11. Willard, p. 108.
12. Martha Thatcher, "Hearing God's Voice," *Discipleship Journal* 37 (1987), p. 45.
13. E. Glenn Hinson, "Making the Most of the Time," *Weavings* 6, no. 1 (January-February 1991), p. 43.

Chapter Fourteen: Being Present for Others
1. Eugene Peterson, *The Contemplative Pastor* (Grand Rapids: Eerdmans, 1989), p. 43.
2. Henri Nouwen, *The Way of the Heart* (San Francisco: HarperSanFrancisco, 1991), p. 63.
3. Richard Foster, *Freedom of Simplicity* (San Francisco: Harper and Row, 1981), p. 84.
4. Gerrit S. Dawson, "Feasts in the Desert and Other Unlikely Places," *Weavings* 9, no. 1 (January-February 1994), p. 33.

Chapter Fifteen: Removing Stones in the Path
1. Susan Howatch, *Absolute Truths* (New York: Knopf, 1995), p. 169.
2. Dallas Willard, *In Search of Guidance: Developing a Conversational Relationship with God* (San Francisco: HarperSanFrancisco, 1993), p. 92.
3. A. W. Tozer, *The Pursuit of God* (Camp Hill, Pa.: Christian Publications, 1982), p. 45.
4. John Baillie, *A Diary of Private Prayer* (New York: Collier, 1977), p. 75.

Chapter Sixteen: Addressing Deeper Fears About God
1. C. S. Lewis, *The Last Battle* (New York: Collier, 1976), p. 16.
2. C. S. Lewis, *The Lion, the Witch, and the Wardrobe* (New York: Collier, 1976), pp. 75-76.

Chapter Seventeen: Believing God Loves Me

1. Henri Nouwen, "Forgiveness: The Name of Love in a Wounded World," *Weavings* 7, no. 2 (March-April 1992), pp. 8-9. These thoughts are more fully developed in Nouwen's book, *The Life of the Beloved* (New York: Crossroad, 1992).
2. A. W. Tozer, *The Pursuit of God* (Camp Hill, Pa.: Christian Publications, 1982), p. 64.
3. Curt Grayson and Jan Johnson, *Healing Hurts That Sabotage the Soul* (Wheaton, Ill.: Victor, 1995), p. 183.

Chapter Eighteen: Revamping the "Quiet Time"

1. Reprinted from *Just for a Moment, I Saw the Light* by John Duckworth (Wheaton, Ill.: Victor Books, SP Publications, Inc., 1994), pp. 198-202. Used by permission.
2. Dallas Willard, *The Spirit of the Disciplines* (San Francisco: Harper and Row, 1988), pp. 3-4.
3. Henri Nouwen, *The Way of the Heart* (San Francisco: Harper-SanFrancisco, 1991), p. 37.
4. Richard Foster, *Celebration of Discipline* (San Francisco: Harper and Row, 1988), pp. 30-31.
5. Brother Lawrence, *The Practice of the Presence of God* (Old Tappan, N.J.: Revell, 1958), p. 31.
6. Jack R. Taylor, *The Hallelujah Factor* (Nashville: Broadman, 1983), pp. 24, 25.
7. Evelyn Underhill, *Renovare Devotional Readings*, ed. James B. Smith, vol. 1, no. 15 (Wichita, Kan.: Renovare, 1990), p. 2.
8. Brother Lawrence, pp. 36-37.

Epilogue: What to Expect on Your Journey

1. Brother Lawrence, *The Practice of the Presence of God* (Old Tappan, N.J.: Revell, 1958), p. 34.
2. Frank Laubach, *Man of Prayer*, The Heritage Collection (Syracuse, N.Y.: Laubach Literacy International, 1990), p. 240.
3. Jean Nicholas Grou, *Renovare Devotional Readings*, ed. James B. Smith, vol. 1, no. 5 (Wichita, Kan.: Renovare, 1990), pp. 1-2.
4. Brother Lawrence, p. 17.
5. Richard Foster, *Prayer: Finding the Heart's True Home* (San Francisco: HarperSanFrancisco, 1992), p. 128.
6. Laubach, p. 250.
7. Tilden Edwards, *Living in the Presence: Disciplines of the Spiritual Heart* (San Francisco: Harper and Row, 1987), p. ix, quoting Dom John Chapman, location not cited.
8. Frank C. Laubach, *Channels of Spiritual Power* (Westwood, N.J.: Revell, 1954), pp. 96-97.
9. Laubach, *Channels of Spiritual Power*, p. 97.

MORE HELP FROM JAN JOHNSON FOR A DEEPER CONNECTION WITH GOD .

Listening to God

With fifty-two topically arranged meditations on real-life themes, *Listening to God* moves meditation out of the realm of mystics and makes this important spiritual discipline accessible for everyday believers.